A
TREE
IN THE
HOUSE

A TREE IN THE HOUSE

ANNABELLE HICKSON

Hardie Grant

BOOKS

CONTENTS

WHY FLOWERS?

•

ONE OF THE GREATEST JOYS OF PLAYING AND EXPERIMENTING with flowers is that it opens your eyes to the beautiful things growing around you. The ones that are already there, doing their thing, that you didn't have to buy or water or prune. You start to notice them. Like words whose meaning you've just learnt (*nadir* and *akimbo*), you start, as if by magic, to see them everywhere.

And the more you think about flowers on the home front, the more you start to see the outside world through a kind of flower filter. You pay attention to what nature is doing around you, and even to bits and pieces beyond the natural world. Old, rusty buckets morph from junk destined for the tip into the perfect vessel for the mass of jasmine hanging over Mr Smith's fence, which you will pinch in the dead of night.

There are writers who say that one of the greatest unexpected consequences of writing is that you become a better reader. Just as, I would say, playing and working with flowers can help you become a better observer of the natural world. Anything that helps you focus on what is beautiful and interesting in your daily life, when so much can feel repetitive and mundane and ordinary, is worthy of celebration. Reverence, even.

So if, like me, there is a terse and rather annoying voice in your head that often yells 'Put down the flowers and do something useful with your life', just ignore her and her arms akimbo. Continue to remove the thorns from your rose stem knowing you are onto a good thing – a practice that can bring meaning, beauty and cause for celebration into your everyday (and into that of those around you).

You do not have to be a trained florist to *do*, as Constance Spry would say, *the flowers*. I certainly am not. I have come to flowers and foliage simply because I love to look at them, to touch and smell them. I am greedy for them and I want them to be part of my life. I want them to fill my kitchen and adorn my world for celebrations big and small. And because I don't have a full-time florist on hand to execute my vision, I've taken on the role of the on-staff florist myself. And let me tell you, I have not encountered a single stern-faced, cross-armed gatekeeper along the way saying, 'Mrs Hickson, drop the dahlias – you are simply not qualified for this'. Just as you do not have to be a trained chef to cook delicious things at home, so too is the world of domestic florality open to anyone keen to give it a go.

What follows are tips for making arrangements and installations in the style I personally like: a little wild, asymmetrical, whimsical and enormous wherever possible. Keep in mind that nothing has to be complicated to be good. A mass of any one thing looks amazing ... four bunches of supermarket daisies, taken out of their plastic and bundled together in an old ceramic jug, are a joy to behold. One single, fragrant gardenia in a tiny vase beside your bed is the height of sophistication. But I digress ...

ON FALLING IN LOVE WITH A PLACE

Anyone who likes to dream knows expectations can often be so high that reality becomes dreadfully disappointing. This flaw of mine was at its worst before we came to where we live now: on a pecan farm in an isolated, narrow valley in north-west New South Wales.

I was based in a rural town further west, where I had moved from a city life as a journalist after falling in love with a farmer. We bought a beautiful, enormous weatherboard house that was borderline derelict. I dreamt we would restore it and live happily ever after. I honestly pictured myself wandering around in white linen, surrounded by beauty and filled with happiness, and children with forever-clean faces playing happily with wooden toys. But the reality was a huge, costly project with blown-out budgets and mounting stress. My husband and I fought a lot. My daughter's preschool teacher pulled me aside one day and asked if there was trouble on the home front. We finished the lengthy project, but it just about killed us. And it was a far cry from the dream this city slicker had about life in the country. Who thinks of the words 'mortgage' and 'therapy' when they are planning their bucolic vegie patch?

Throughout the renovating process we would go over to the valley, where we had started a small pecan plantation, to spend weekends in the tiny, simple cottage on the hill before returning to our 'dream' house. We never wanted to leave, but did because we thought we should. After all, we had custom joinery to return to. Isn't that what we had wanted? But slowly, the idea grew that we really could stay; we really could simplify our lives.

And we did. We put the big house on the market, packed up all our stuff and took what can only be called a capsule collection of belongings to the charmless cottage with aluminium windows in desperate need of a paint job. I finally let go of what I thought would make me happy and swapped it for what was actually making me happy, in real life, already.

I had hoped for a less stressful life in this little valley – financially and mentally – but I did not anticipate the overwhelming joy. The sense of awe that would wash over me like a wave on the beach even at the most ordinary of times, like hanging the washing out on the line with the sky above, cockatoos squawking in the distance and me just a tiny speck on the grass. The yellow and purple weeds flowering among the bleached-out tall grasses. The majestic gum trees.

And because I felt good, I started to look outwards rather than always in, in, in. I saw things I hadn't noticed before. Growing things. Pale green gum leaves, purple poppies and blackberries on the side of the road. Swaying tall stands of wild fennel.

I started bringing wildflowers into the house to spruce up the drab rooms with their tobacco-yellow walls, and sprigs of eucalyptus to hang off the shower head. And then I got into gardening, if you call chucking a few cosmos seeds into some holes gardening. But you can, because before too long those seeds morphed into towers of pink and white flower heads that waved in the wind by the kitchen window. It felt very empowering. With very little expense I could dig a hole, plant the seeds and, lo and behold, be surrounded by beauty.

Above: Surrounded by tall grass, flowering weeds and my children, Daisy, Harriet and Tom, in the paddock in-between our house and the pecan orchard.
Right: Barefoot children – how their feet can handle all the spiky burs I do not know – having morning tea under the tower of teddy bear sunflowers in the kitchen.
Below: The rogue chooks who sleep in the fig tree next to the kitchen by night, and try to sneak into the house by day.

Crocosmia and vines – held in place by a metal flower frog –
exploding out of a bowl, in among the kitchen chaos at home.

Top left: My husband, Ed, holding a bunch of cotton he has grown, just before the big harvest begins.
Above: An explosion of fennel fireworks in the kitchen.
Right: The kids, my beloved Newfoundland dog, Pommes Frites, and me, walking to the mailbox to see what the postman has brought this week.
Left: A gang of children on their way to the top of the mountain overlooking the pecan orchard.

Soon enough my hovel of a house, which I could vacuum in its entirety from the one power plug, was dripping with natural beauty. Luxurious, affordable, compostable splendour. I could use what was growing around me to create living vignettes; temporary tableaux of wilting vines spilling down from the shelf above the laundry sink, or a mini collection of different gum leaves in a cluster of vases on the kitchen table. More by default than by design, the things filling the vases in my kitchen were a microcosmic reflection of what was happening in the macro world outside. And without any conscious effort, I began to experience a deep and steady sense of connection to the environment around me.

For some reason, this place felt like home before it was. Even now, three years on from our official move here, I still feel lucky. All that joy hasn't been deadened by daily life. I feel embraced by this landscape.

That is why I love flowers. Or more broadly, things that grow.

And they grow everywhere. We have a prickly pear growing in the crook of an enormous gum tree, where a branch meets the trunk at least 15 metres up in the air. There is a laneway next to the butcher's shop in town where a vigorous clump of nasturtiums lives happily. The butcher lets me pick as many as I want, and I make a nasturtium butter with the leaves and flowers and give him a rounded, green-flecked butter pat as thanks. (I don't know if he eats it; he's never told me.) A friend who lives in a city terrace grows her annuals in wheelbarrows, which she wheels out onto the verge every morning to harvest the sun.

But beyond what we intentionally grow, there is so much out there that grows naturally. There is such abundance in the natural world.

Norwegian writer Karl Ove Knausgaard speaks so beautifully about this force in his book *Autumn*, recounting how he stood back to look at an apple tree he had pruned with a heavy hand:

'Maimed was the word that came to mind. But the branches have grown back, densely covered with leaves, and the tree is loaded with apples. That's the experience I've had with working in the garden: there's no reason to be anxious or cautious about anything, life is so robust, it seems to come cascading, blind and green, and at times it is frightening, because we too are alive, but we live in what amounts to a controlled environment, which makes us fear what is blind, wild, chaotic, stretching towards the sun, but most often also beautiful, in a deeper way than purely visual, for the soil smells of rot and darkness, teems with scuttling beetles and convulsing worms, the flower stalks are juicy, their petals brim with scents, and the air, cold and sharp, warm and humid, filled with sunrays or rain, lies against the skin, accustomed to the indoors, like a soothing compress of hereness.'

A soothing compress of hereness: this is what flowers are to me. And this is why I want them to be wild and thorny and richly scented. I want them to speak of the rotting dark soil from which they came and the harsh sun they grew under. I want them to drop their crunchy leaves on my floor. I am not interested in perfectly thornless, scentless hothouse-grown flowers flown in from the other side of the world. I want to feel them coming at me, cascading, blind and green. Wild and chaotic and sure. To me, this is beauty.

01

FLOWER BASICS

BEGINNING TO THINK ABOUT FLOWERS

•

'In the use of flowers for the decoration of her house, the modern woman may find her artist's material. The creative urge is strong in us and among the strong emotions of the human heart is a love of beauty and a desire to create beauty. But it is not given to all of us to be artists in the generally accepted sense of the word. With flowers, however, with living plants as your medium, it is possible to create beauty, even to the degree of making a masterpiece. Quickly I want to say that this joyful experience is not limited to those of you who can grow or buy rare and expensive flowers, but is for everyone, schoolchild or student, town or countrywoman, for everyone who loves a beautiful thing and will take a little trouble.'

- CONSTANCE SPRY, IN HER DELIGHTFUL BOOK *HOW TO DO THE FLOWERS*
(which I cannot recommend highly enough)

IF I COULD PRINT CONSTANCE SPRY'S 1953 BOOK *How to Do the Flowers* here in full, I would. It is not a big book, but it is a thoughtful one, and full of very good information. It is this book that first got me thinking about 'arranging' flowers, as opposed to simply plonking them in a vase.

Ms Spry, in between singing the praises of chicken wire and allotments ('strange that so good a thing should come out of war'), wrote – very usefully – about the line of an arrangement: the shape of the outline of the arrangement as a whole, including the vase, and the visual lines of movement within it. I had not consciously thought about this before, but now it is all I can do when I look at a flower arrangement. I put an imaginary frame around the arrangement and seek out diagonally cascading lines, from top left to right bottom or vice versa. I look for different heights and depths, I search for little undulations of light and shadow. And if you keep this in mind while arranging, it can feel like painting. I was never any good at painting, but always wanted to be. Now, instead of worrying about paint on a canvas, the flowers are my brush strokes. It is the most instantly gratifying form of art that I know.

What follows are some thoughts on how to prepare your flowers, how to make them last, how to support them in a vessel, but most importantly, how to think about your arrangements as a work of art, in the spirit of Ms Spry.

FINDING FLOWERS

I very much believe that free flowers are the best flowers.

If, like me, you are greedy for flowers, you will have to explore ways of getting your mitts on them beyond simply buying them. Unless, of course, you have very deep pockets, but in that case you'll miss out on half the fun.

Grow your flowers if you can. It's a bit hard if you live in a high-rise or in cities like Sydney and New York, where the cost of real estate per square metre makes my chest involuntarily tighten. But once you start looking, you'll be surprised what you might find. For my father-in-law's birthday party, I decked out a boating shed overlooking the Sydney Harbour Bridge with branches of wattle picked from alongside the city railway line. It looked fabulous and cost nothing.

In Britain in the summertime you almost can't pass a railway line without seeing a flowering buddleia. These perennials love a good prune and, although their flowers won't last more than three days in a vase, the sheer number of them means you can cut again and again.

Never take too many branches from any one tree or shrub – I'd always leave at least two-thirds so as not to overly stress it. And remember, a clean cut on an angle is much better for the tree than snapping and ripping off branches and stems.

Keep your eyes peeled for vegetation along roadsides and in abandoned lots, laneways and, of course, in the countryside. Don't discount weeds. Foliage, grasses, gumnuts, branches, vines ... so much is out there for the picking. And if you cannot find these things close to home, I would argue it is time to get out of the city for a mini-break.

Keep some secateurs in your glove box and an old blanket in the boot, and stop when you see something that catches your eye. Screech to a halt if you have to; ignore the complaints of your husband and friends. Knock on doors and ask if you can cut a stem or a branch. Most people with gorgeous gardens are dying for an opportunity to talk about their roses' first flush or their mulching techniques.

If you have an established garden (I do not. Instead, I watch the little seedlings in the ground like the tired mother watches the kettle boil, and still so many of them perish), pruning and cutting back seems like a major job, even if it is one I dream about. But this trash can become your treasure. I think we need a floral cuttings app along the lines of Tinder, which can match up those with excess branches with those who want to hang them from the ceiling. Swipe right if you want the gorgeous camellia branches.

And of course, do buy flowers if your budget allows. I very much like the idea of supporting flower farmers and florists, particularly local ones.

A word of caution, though: I find that I am overly precious with bought flowers. I worry about cutting them in case I go too short; I worry about damaging them if I decide to start the arrangement again. Basically, I am overly anxious with them in ways that can get in the way of creativity and spontaneity. The stench of my concern can leech its way onto the arrangements and they can feel a bit, I don't know, *stressed* instead of whimsical. So, if you are like me, sit yourself down and say, 'For goodness sake, we are not curing world poverty here. The stakes aren't that high. You've already blown your dough, so just have fun'.

Above: Daisy and me in a field of cosmos at a friend's house.
Left & below: Daisy collecting weeds and wildflowers on the farm.
Right: A ute filled with chestnut branches, cut from one of the neighbour's chestnut trees.

FLOWER TO VASE PROPORTIONS

For some, this piece of advice will be completely obvious, while for others, it may be the single most important thing to keep in mind when arranging anything in a vase.

When you look at an arrangement as a whole, from the bottom of the vase to the top of the leaves, you want to see two-thirds plant material and one-third vase. Or, at the very least, half and half. I very much like arrangements that take these proportions even further: say four-fifths plant material, one-fifth vase. But almost always, when there is more vase than plant material, I am disappointed. It's like microwaved bacon. There's just no need for it.

Some people struggle with this at the classes I teach, but when they learn to see their arrangements this way it's as if a light has been switched on and their arrangements instantly jump up a level.

DO

DON'T

Here we have the same glass cylindrical vase and plant material – basil – but two very different looks. Above you have two-thirds basil, one-third vase, where the basil flows from the top left to the bottom right, cascading over the vase's lip. There is an airiness that feels very natural. Your eye is taken from left to right, top to bottom, down a visual river.

Look at this depressing blob that is two-thirds vase, one-third basil. There is no movement or air in the way the basil stems have been arranged – just a stagnant lump in a vase that is way too big for it, like a small foot in an oversized sandal.

DO

Here we have a tiny vase of cosmos flowers. The proportions are great and the cosmos sit naturally in the vase.

DON'T

In this arrangement, we have more vase than cosmos, leaving us with an unnatural, uninspiring lump.

DO

This arrangement of a single rose works well – the flower head and foliage are beautifully in proportion to the vase.

DON'T

This rose is cut way too short. Instead of gracefully emerging up and out of the vase, it looks stunted.

Here is an example of the proportion of vase to plant material squeezed right down.
I absolutely love it, especially with light flowers or foliage, such as this Queen Anne's lace, that grow tall like this in nature.

PREPPING YOUR VESSEL

For single-vase arrangements, I love to use opaque vessels with relatively wide openings – urns, bowls, soup tureens and footed bowls – as opposed to the more common tall vases with their narrow mouths. The width of these vessels allows the flowers to poke out at great angles, almost horizontally (something you cannot do with a tall, narrow vase), which allows for some really interesting arrangements and visual rivers that your eye naturally wants to follow.

However, when using wider vessels, you will need to create a structure within them to prevent the flowers from flopping and falling out. This is very easy, thanks to chicken wire and floral tape. Keep in mind when using chicken wire that you should stick to opaque vessels, as you don't want to see the wire and mess of stems woven into it. And remember, a vessel is anything that can hold water, from a rusty old 40-gallon drum to a thimble. You can even make leaky vessels, such as a wooden crate, watertight by lining them with thick black plastic sheeting from the hardware shop, cut to size and secured with floral tape.

Choose your vessel and make sure it's clean. Cut a generous piece of chicken wire with wire cutters, or a pair of secateurs that you don't care about (as the wire will rough up the blades). For added stability, fix a flower frog to the bottom of the vessel with floral putty before you add the chicken wire. It will take the weight of any particularly heavy branches.

Loosely concertina the chicken wire, folding it up like an accordion to form at least three or four layers, then gently ball it up and stuff it into your vessel. Using several layers of chicken wire will give you more holes to weave the stems through, stabilising the flowers so they won't flop around. You want the folded wire to fill the vessel generously so that it rises just above the lip (pictured opposite). It might take a couple of goes to get the size of the chicken wire to correspond with the size of the vessel, but once your eye is in, you'll have no trouble.

If the fit is tight enough, with the wire touching the inside of the vessel all the way around, you may not have to secure it with floral tape. But as my chicken wire balls are often imperfect, I create a floral tape grid to secure the wire in place. Without the grid, the chicken wire might fall all over the place when you add the flower stems, making arranging tricky. To secure it, just fix the end of your floral tape to the lip of the bowl and pull it across tightly, pressing down on the top of the chicken wire ball, and fix it to the opposite side of the bowl, tearing it off just over the lip. Repeat this process to make a grid (pictured opposite), which will keep the mound of chicken wire steady as you insert stems. You can hide the tape clinging to the lip of the vessel with bits of foliage in your arrangement.

Now fill the vessel with some fresh, flower-friendly water. Here is a recipe for some (care of CSIRO's *Caring for Cut Flowers* manual, which is very informative about this sort of stuff). It's just like sprinkling in one of those flower food sachets.

FLOWER-FRIENDLY WATER

1 litre (34 fl oz/4 cups) water

¼ teaspoon bleach (4% concentration)

2 teaspoons sugar

1 teaspoon vinegar

Pour the water into a vase, then add the bleach, sugar and vinegar.

The bleach kills the bacteria and other clogging germs, the sugar feeds the flowers, and the acid in the vinegar makes it easier for the flowers to suck up the sugary water, which is thicker than normal water and therefore harder to drink.

TOP
___

Wide, open vessels like this large ceramic-footed bowl allow for wonderful arrangements with lots of angles, but you need to create a structure to secure the flowers in place. Here, I have used a large metal flower frog, stuck to the bottom of the bowl with floral putty (which is like a waterproof adhesive putty), and topped it with a large multi-layered ball of chicken wire.

BOTTOM
___

The structure is secured in place with a floral tape grid over the lip of the bowl to provide a sturdy support for the flowers about to be added to the arrangement. By opting for this full array of flower securing devices, you will be able to steady even large, top-heavy branches, such as this enormous spray of roses.

COLOUR AND SELECTION

When selecting flowers to arrange, stick to a palette. Don't just jam in all the pretties within reach, which can be hard to resist when you have gorgeous blue delphiniums, yellow garden roses and pink salvias all flowering at the same time. Much like choosing an outfit, an arrangement's success comes just as much from what you choose *not* to put in.

I like to work with colours that are close to each other on the colour wheel rather than opposite. I adore buff tones with apricots and browns, pinks with purples or reds, and yellows with whites. You may have different preferences, but it is worthwhile to start with a limited colour scheme, playing around and moving on from there. If you are working with sweeter colours, such as bright pinks and yellows, it's often a good idea to add a bit of brown or a colour with a bit of dirt in it to tone the arrangement down. Brisbane interior designer Anna Spiro, whose work is much loved for her use of bright colours and patterns, swears by adding a touch of brown. I think this wisdom translates to flowers as well.

English gardener and writer Christopher Lloyd, who created one of the most beautiful – and perhaps unconventional – gardens in England, believed firmly in the benefits of taking risks with colour, advocating the combination of supposedly clashing colours such as orange and magenta. And then there is that ridiculous saying that *blue and green should never be seen*. What a load of rubbish! All you have to do is look out the window and see the green grass and the blue sky to know that it is meaningless. The moral of the story is to work with the colours you like and not let the pursuit of 'good taste' stop you from experimenting.

With your colour palette at the forefront of your mind, choose some flowers to work with, along with some foliage and other textural pieces, like grass or branches with berries. Any little bits you can pick from the side of the road or a garden will really help give the arrangement a more natural, wild-and-woolly vibe. Then, as if you were a very important Parisian florist, clear the decks of the most suitable table you own, gently pile the flowers and foliage upon it, get some snips and prepare some clean buckets filled one-third of the way up with water.

In this arrangement, the buff tones of the grasses, along with the dried gum leaves, mix beautifully with the soft pinks of the dried bougainvillea in the back and the fluffy pink peonies and pink and red garden roses in the foreground.

A classic Hodgean arrangement. My favourite florist, Sarah Hodge, has created a thing of beauty here. With only a few vines of a purple-flowering clematis and some old, wispy manuka branches, she has created a wild explosion that looks like it has ever so naturally grown out of the gold-coloured bowl below. She used chicken wire in the bowl and secured it in place with floral tape. Tucked into the back left of the arrangement, down low, are a couple of light purple bearded irises – a reward for the careful observer.

PREPPING YOUR FLOWERS

When it comes to cooking, I am a chop-on-demand kind of girl, but with flowers I like to have them all prepped and ready before I start arranging. I like putting the flowers together quickly, before I have a chance to overthink them, and this process is much helped if I have already cleaned up the stems – but, by all means, do what works best for you when you arrange your flowers.

To prep your flowers, trim off the bottom leaves on each stem – any leaves that would sit below the water line in your vase need to go because they will soil the water and reduce the vase life of the material in it – and make a fresh diagonal cut at the bottom of each stem before putting them in a bucket of water, ready to be used in your arrangement. The diagonal cut increases the surface area of the stem, which helps with water uptake. It also stops any stems from sitting flush on the bottom of the vessel, which would make it hard for them to drink the water.

You can easily remove the thorns from rose stems by holding the rose near the head with your non-dominant hand. Then, with your other hand, clutch the stem near the head with a face cloth or thick tea towel folded in half and pull it down the stem, bringing the thorns with you.

CREATING A BASE

Start by creating the general shape of your arrangement with a foliage base. You might want to thin it out a bit by snipping off some leaves; you don't want it to look too heavy. Angle pieces into a more-or-less central spot in the chicken wire, coming out at different angles and depths. It is really helpful to keep this spot in mind as you arrange, imagining that the flowers should all explode like a firework from that point. I particularly love an asymmetrical explosion, with a high side on the left, a low side on the right (or vice versa) and some negative space in the middle.

The master of this high-side, low-side arrangement style is Sarah Hodge, a remarkable florist and grower from New Zealand who works under the name Horrobin and Hodge. She manages to inject incredible movement into her arrangements (like the one pictured at left). It is as if the flowers and foliage have been frozen in time, mid-swirl, as opposed to artificially fixed into place in a static scene forevermore. This is the mood I try to create – not always with success, but the intention is there.

Make sure you hide some of the vessel's lip as you go, by allowing some foliage to spill over it. I really don't like seeing the entire rim of a vessel.

ARRANGING

Now that you have your shape and base, work in groups of three of the same flower. For example, roses: stagger in groups of three, aiming for pockets of colour. Then add some bigger flowers, like peonies or dahlias. It is much more effective to create a pop of three roses grouped together than just one, especially in larger arrangements. It makes me particularly happy when these pockets of colour form rivers, flowing their way through different heights and depths. Keep in mind that not every single flower head needs to face forward; this is not a school photo. It looks much more interesting when flowers face in different directions, as they do in nature.

Dot through some texture – little berries or small, delicate, floaty flowers that feel light and airy – to soften the pockets of colour formed by other, larger flowers.

Stand back and gaze at your arrangement as you go. Some people like to work on a lazy Susan so they can rotate the arrangement as they work. It is very easy to ignore one side, so I see the advantage of this, but I just work on the end of a table.

Don't be scared to stop. It is so much easier to add more than to take away. Place the arrangement in situ and see how it feels; you may find yourself looking at it from a different angle. I almost always add something at this point.

So many words of instruction; they are for the pedants among us (if you are a pedant and have not read Julian Barnes's *A Pedant in the Kitchen*, you must immediately. It will be a wonderfully validating experience). For the more philistine florists – hello, sisters – all you really need to keep in mind is this: asymmetrical rivers of colour. Diagonal movement within the arrangement. Different heights, different depths, different shapes, all exploding from a central point in the vase. And just as we are told not to crowd the pan when cooking mushrooms, let the flowers have some air to breathe too.

The following chapter is filled with flowers-in-the-house inspiration for throughout the year. Some are tiny arrangements; others are a mass of one thing – the options are endless.

A tight bunch of roses on the left contrasts with an airier arrangement of dahlias on the right. I've stuffed some chicken wire into the jug on the right, which allows the dahlias to stand in place, while still allowing a little movement. Flower foam – or Oasis as it is commonly known – would also hold the flowers up, but has the dispiriting disadvantages of allowing zero movement and being carcinogenic.

02

FLOWERS AT HOME

A TABLEAU VIVANT OF THE DAILY

•

I AM VERY SUSPICIOUS OF PEOPLE WHO DON'T THINK TO put a sprig of something in a vase around their house. My husband is one of those people. If he didn't live with me, hell would freeze over before a bunch of dill in a jar found its way onto the kitchen table, or a vignette of gum leaves covering the old wood oven and the wall it sits in front of.

I keep an eye on him, half expecting a sleek spaceship to one day land in the backyard and take him back to his place of origin: a planet where pets don't require any care from their owners and there is no such thing as a vase.

Although I am dedicated to this man, I cannot imagine what it must feel like to walk past a flowering weed and not want to pick some to take back home, to the Airbnb, car, doctor's surgery, or wherever I am headed. I want to cut it all. (Arguably, this represents a psychological issue of its own, but if you are reading this I think it is fair to say we're bonkers in the same way and we can agree to categorise non-vase-filling people as the aliens they are.)

Occasionally, I try to sate the desire to be surrounded by natural things by potting up a few house plants, but, alas, remembering to water them is not always easy. The cat likes to shred them for reasons I cannot understand. And when they die, I feel terribly selfish and irresponsible. Much better, in my view, to snip a few bits and pieces from plants outside that won't mind the haircut, and that you can watch wither and wilt without remorse.

Here are some suggestions for when it comes to making arrangements for around the house. Not for the table where you are eating – I have some uncharacteristically definite views on that (page 104) – but for sideboards, on top of fireplace mantles, or in a corner of the kitchen. For when you want something more complex than a bunch of the same type of flower in a jug. For when you want to recreate a micro version of what is growing in the macro world outside. To use American author Donna Tartt's words, for when you want to create 'a tableau vivant of the daily'.

First, you must choose to make either one single arrangement in a single vessel or a visual tableau using several vessels to form the one arrangement. The aim of both is to use the plant material to create rivers of movement at different heights and depths throughout the arrangement.

And remember, if you can't be bothered to think about creating rivers or vignettes or anything fancy, fear not. Something as simple as a couple of sprigs of rosemary in a little glass bottle is all it takes to bring a bit of the outside in. To connect our controlled, interior lives with that of the great outdoors. To remind us that spring will come after winter again and again and again. I think that is why I like flowers in the house so much. They are a gentle reminder that there are things much larger than my own finite life buzzing all around me, all the time.

SINGLE-VASE ARRANGEMENTS

It's hard to beat a single, fragrant rose in a well-proportioned vase or a bunch of tulips piled so that they gracefully flop over one side. Why overcomplicate matters by doing anything more? But just as there are times when I feel compelled to prepare a huge Sunday evening feast complete with pudding as opposed to an egg on toast, there are times when I want to create something a little more complicated than a bloom in a bud vase. One is not better than the other – they are simply different approaches.

Here are some thoughts for when you are in the mood to create an arrangement of several types of flowers and foliage. When you want to get a bit fancy. After all, there are some incredible things you can do in a single vase, particularly when you use wide, open vessels – such as a ceramic mixing bowl – and employ a few tricks (see page 28) to help the flowers defy the laws of gravity.

David Austin roses, peppered with floaty pink cosmos and Japanese anemones, springing out of a ceramic vase stuffed with chicken wire.

A large white enamel bowl, filled with chicken wire taped into place with floral tape, holds a glorious spring ensemble of philadelphus (mock orange) branches, snowball viburnums, pink wisteria, pink statice, some delicate sprigs of purple-flowering clematis and some purple irises.

LEFT

Six elegant stems of white Japanese anenomes sprouting out of a ceramic jug, held in place with a ball of chicken wire. I love the lean to the right – it's as if they are ever so slightly sighing.

RIGHT

A joyous cluster of apricot-coloured Crepuscule roses, amassed in a jug filled with chicken wire to hold them in place. What a welcome sight when you are weary of washing dishes.

ABOVE

A small, globe-shaped ceramic vase filled with pink syngonium leaves, flowering sedum, roses, grass stems and the blue stems of *Salvia azurea*.

RIGHT

This white ceramic-footed bowl is the perfect vessel for large arrangements such as this spilling array of roses. The vessel's weight prevents it from toppling over, while a flower frog, chicken wire and a floral tape grid keep the roses in place.

LEFT

I absolutely adore this combination of pinks and reds. Here, the delicate plum blossoms sing in among the red and pink spring roses and the dark chocolate cosmos. I removed all green leaves from the stems to exaggerate the feeling of light and air in the arrangement.

ABOVE LEFT

Apricot, pale pink and buff tones blend together beautifully in this rose and grass arrangement. A ball of chicken wire in the ceramic bowl keeps the flowers in their places.

ABOVE RIGHT

The bright contrast of pink cyclamens, purple clematis and white iceberg roses creates a joyful autumn arrangement.

A rusty bucket filled with chicken wire, a base of flowering ironbark eucalypt, and a peppering of pink and red garden roses.

Lichen-covered branches collected from the side of the road in winter will happily sit in a vase for months.

ANNE ENRIGHT THE GREEN ROAD

AUTUMN KARL OVE KNAUSGAARD

A Writing Life Helen Garner and Her Work
Bernadette Brennan

MEG
MASON *You be Mother*

OSTRO · Julia Busuttil Nishimura

LEFT
_____

A winter explosion of lemon branches in an old wooden pail. The pail itself is not waterproof, so hidden inside it is a cylindrical glass vase (stuffed with chicken wire) to hold the water.

ABOVE
_____

This small, handmade ceramic bowl, which I like to eat my porridge out of, makes for a great vase. Here, with a flower frog secured to its bottom, it becomes the perfect container for a cascading arrangement of evening primrose flowers, dried allium and poppy heads, and the flowering weed Paterson's curse.

ABOVE

A group of foxglove spires high on the left, the verdant vines from a Virginia creeper spilling down and over the right, and some delicate purple clematis stems snaking their way around the centre make for a joyful summer arrangement in a white enamel jug.

RIGHT

Fragrant garden roses, peppered through with grass seed heads and white cosmos, arranged in the shape of a love heart, decorate a bedroom.

LEFT

Just when winter starts to feel too bleak, the incredibly fragrant wintersweet blooms. Here are a few branches winding their way out of a copper jug on a friend's farmhouse verandah.

ABOVE

I find proteas quite hard to work with – their stiff, thick, unyielding stems make me think of rigor mortis – but here, in among the autumn branches and the last of summer's red fairy roses, they provide a lovely pinky-red textural heart to the arrangement.

'DAHLIAS ARE A BIT LIKE WINSTON CHURCHILL OR JOHN TRAVOLTA. THEY TOO HAVE HAD WILDERNESS YEARS WHEN NOBODY REALLY UNDERSTOOD THEM AND THEY FLOUNDERED ABOUT, FAILING TO FULFIL THEIR FULL POTENTIAL.'

- JAMES ALEXANDER-SINCLAIR

DAHLIAS:
THE WORKING-CLASS FLOWER

•

The dahlia was very popular in Europe from the 1830s onwards, after arriving on European shores from Mexico. But by the 1960s it had become, as British garden designer and writer Noel Kingsbury matter-of-factly says, a 'working-class flower'. What on earth *is* a working-class flower? Sometimes it must be awful to be British.

Does it mean a flower for the poor – for those who don't have a staff and must tend to the garden themselves? If so, speaking from personal experience, the dahlia is very well suited to the working class. I do nothing to mine, save for watering them, and they produce bloom after joyful bloom. I am reminded of that phrase: 'If you want to feel loved, get a dog. If you want to feel really loved, get two'. Sub in 'dahlia' for 'dog' and you will understand how they make me feel.

Or does 'working-class flower' mean one for those with poor taste? Something naff, if not vulgar, like the scorned carnation, chrysanthemum and gladioli?

Semantics aside, from around the 1960s until very recently, the dahlia fell out of favour with everyone except the men who grew them as specimens to enter into flower shows. Or those with bad taste.

Gardener Christopher Lloyd of Great Dixter in England, known by some as the King of Clash and by others as a courageous, innovative gardener, did much to bring the dahlia back into vogue. He considered the phrase 'good taste' a bad one. He ripped out the old, formal rose garden at Great Dixter to make way for an exotic garden full of dahlias and cannas and banana trees.

And now they are all the rage again. In late summer, Instagram is flooded with images of muted wedding bouquets of soft Cafe au Laits and ute-loads of buckets bursting with brightly coloured dahlias. And while their colours may be shouting at each other, to paraphrase Lloyd, they are shouting for joy. I really can't imagine scoffing at such glorious, joyful beauty. But I probably would have if I was born a couple of decades earlier.

I think poor geraniums and pelargoniums might still fall in the working-class category for some (although those geranium-scented Aesop handwashes have done a lot to improve their image). They, too, are easy to grow, and they tirelessly produce flowers throughout the season.

We must examine our prejudices, at least every now and then. How much are we writing off because it is not trendy? What are we overlooking now? No flower should be ignored. Not even the agapanthus, which I can barely bring myself to look at. I hate her in a way that is both completely unjustified and cruel. She's condemned in my mind for being dependable, long flowering and – worst of all – suburban. Gawd, I am no better than the dahlia snobs!

Top: A mix of different types of dahlias – cactus, decorative and ball – stripped of their leaves and cut at different lengths fill a small stone urn and a glass jar.

Bottom: The peach and raspberry tones of this lovely dahlia cloud bring me great joy. Chicken wire allows the stems to hold their place, while the different heights and depths of the flower heads create an interesting contrast of light and shadow within the arrangement.

Pink and red dahlias, along with delicate stems of pink Japanese anemones, fill this concrete urn.
A ball of chicken wire submerged in the urn keeps everything in place.

TABLEAUX: MULTI-VASE ARRANGEMENTS

You can really play with scale when using several vases to create one floral scene. The rivers of colour you can build are obviously much larger than when working with only one vase.

My main piece of advice for multi-vase arrangements is to work with blocks of plant materials. You don't want to have, for example, five single-vase arrangements scattered across a kitchen bench, as the details specific to each individual arrangement will be lost in such a large format. Instead, think of the entire multi-vase arrangement as one arrangement, with each vase a section of it. So instead of scattering gumnuts through different vases, have one vase filled with just gumnuts.

The larger your branches, the heavier you want your vessels to be. Rusty steel urns and concrete pots are terrific for large-scale work. It is also useful to have a collection of glass cylindrical vases of different heights and widths. They blend into the background very easily and do not distract from the lines and movement in your vignettes. You can also create tiny multi-vase arrangements using single stems and small bud vases of different heights.

Another great advantage of multi-vase arrangements is that they look fabulous using just one material, such as gum leaves. The scale has a way of making up for the lack of variety.

Before and after: Place water-filled vases at different heights and depths across a wall, then simply fill with mini explosions of flowers or foliage. Here, I've used gum leaves, and I think the use of just one type of material looks great on this large scale.

ABOVE

A mini tableau – a pixie-proportioned multi-vase arrangement. It is so easy to play with different heights and depths at this scale by pushing vases back and forth on the tabletop and cutting the stems (in this case dahlias and roses) at different lengths.

RIGHT

One day I didn't have much in the way of afternoon tea for when the kids got off the school bus after the long, winding ride home, so instead I thought I'd delight them with a flood of false asters pouring out of the wood stove. They would have preferred cake, but it did make me very happy. I put a ball of chicken wire in the fire box and threaded in the stems before adding more bunches all over the kitchen.

I've been waiting for years – literally – for the gas man to come out to our place and install a proper gas stovetop. Until then, a camping cooker does the trick, particularly when it is surrounded by wisps of roses, cosmos, dried branches and a small potted maidenhair fern.

LEFT

A mix of pink and red dahlias sit on high, above a jug of hot pink cosmos, scabiosas, pink zinnias and Delbard's 'Maurice Utrillo' pink-and-yellow striped roses.

ABOVE

Water cups filled with pink and white dahlias, stripped of their leaves and cut at different heights, flank two jars of homemade cleaning solution of vinegar, water, rosemary and lemon.

NEXT PAGE

My beloved concrete sink in spring, filled with a bucket of purple wisteria on the left, a bucket of Manchurian pear blossoms in the middle, and a bundle of gum leaves and nuts spilling over the right edge. Beats the dishes any day.

Two vases filled with peonies cut at different heights, with the taller stems in the back vase.

An old green milk vat filled with chestnut branches in the corner of the kitchen. This arrangement is made to look much larger by the addition of another vase on top of the wooden dresser, in the corner, which holds more chestnut branches. Our little kitten is busy stalking the fallen nuts in their spiky casings.

LEFT

Sweet peas and roses in old ink wells. Spring incarnate.

ABOVE

I tried to get away with using this gorgeous slender branch wedged in between the ovens as a Christmas tree, but the children revolted. I love the visual line it creates from the top of the room, down across the ovens, back to the dried hydrangeas in the corner and then over to the snippets of roses and cosmos in small vases on the wooden dresser.

ABOVE

Jugs of roadside blossoms, paper daisies and flannel flowers in the background, a smaller jug of fragrant lily-of-the-valley stems in the centre, all surrounded by mounds of banksias on the left and hakea pods on the right.

RIGHT

Branches laden with persimmons fill a cylindrical glass vase on the floor and a rusty old urn sitting on a wooden pedestal to the right, creating a river of persimmons in front of this beautifully textured wall.

03. FLOWERS

FOR A FRIEND

BEYOND THE MIXED BUNCH

•

'Beauty, in other words, lifts life out of the anaesthetising effects of the pedestrian and gives us reason for going on, for being, for ranging beyond our boundaries, for endeavouring always to be more than we are. It enables us to pause in time long enough to remember that some things are worth striving for, that some things are worth doing over and over again until they become their breathless selves.'

- SISTER JOAN CHITTISTER

At Milan Fashion Week, Gigi Hadid was dressed as an enormous bunch of flowers for the Moschino show. Her body was wrapped in a cellophane-like fabric, with a big red bow around her waist. Her face – somehow serious, despite the get-up – popped up among a sea of flower heads. She was a walking, human-sized bouquet. The thing that bothered me most was not the ridiculous outfit, but that the flowers looked like the scentless, standard hothouse ones you pick up as a mixed bunch from your local service station. Gigi's beautiful head popping out of a dreadful mixed bunch.

To give flowers, and to be given them, can be such a wonderful thing. Even terrible mixed bunches from the service station can soften a hard heart. Because of course, it's not so much about the flowers but about the message they send. Having said that, there are so many dreadful mixed bunches out there that require hard-earned money to be handed over in exchange for them that I cannot help but speak up. We can do better.

On the following pages are some thoughts on how to improve upon the supermarket mixed bunch to keep in mind when you next want to surprise a friend. They centre around choosing one type of flower, and one that is in season.

A cloud of pastel-coloured hydrangeas makes a
lovely bunch to give to a friend.

SIMPLE, SEASONAL BEAUTY

There is something so joyful about a bouquet made up of one type of flower. It feels simple and abundant all at once. I think this sense of delight is heightened when the flowers reflect the season around you, where you are right now. A basket of ripe mangos in the middle of summer, or a huge bunch of crabapple blossoms in spring, can absolutely lift life out of the anaesthetising effects of the pedestrian.

I think we all respond in an elemental way to feeling connected with nature's calendar and its seasons, with the wide-open skies and the fresh, clean air. Yet many of us buffer ourselves from this connection. We're all so hell-bent on avoiding inconvenience. Our houses are climatically controlled all year round. If we want to eat avocado, in season or not, we can and we do. And although I am not about to spearhead a campaign for an air-con handbag, I do think keeping ourselves attuned to the change of the seasons, and going without some things during the year, leaves room to focus more fully on, and appreciate, the things whose natural turn in the sun it is.

There's a lot of comfort to be had in admiring what grows in nature, mainly because it has, for the most part, happened without you doing anything. You are not in control. You could stay in bed all autumn long, watching Netflix, and the leaves would still turn and fall off their branches. The buds would still burst in spring. There are forces greater than our own little lives at play here, and I feel relieved, if not comforted, by this.

This is a rather convoluted way of saying that if you are going to give a bunch of flowers to a friend – to surprise them, to comfort them, or show them they are loved – you may as well consider what time of year it is. Why not gift them a little wonder of the natural world around you?

That, to me, is a sure-fire way of avoiding the terrible mixed bunch: a bundle of a single type of flower, herb or foliage that reflects where you are.

There is a wonderfully preachy 1870s article in the British Victorian-era *St. Nicholas Magazine* that has some very definite ideas on flower design, including the use of a limited variety of flowers (as well as avoiding stiffness at all costs and always including a little touch of yellow – that last bit I am not so sure about):

> *'It is better, as a general rule, not to put more than one or two sorts of flowers into the same vase. A great bush with roses and camellias and carnations and feverfew and geraniums growing on it all at once would be a frightful thing to behold; just so a monstrous bouquet made up of all these flowers is meaningless and ugly.'*
>
> *- ST. NICHOLAS MAGAZINE, 1870s*

I was left with two conflicting sentiments after reading it. On the one hand, I wanted to reach for the revolver. Who is this man, spouting condescending flower how-to statements as if they were facts. Seriously, who is anyone to say what is meaningless and ugly? But on the other, I agreed with him.

So it is with a somewhat troubled mind that I advise you, if you plan on taking something to a friend, whether as a hostess gift or a little pick-me-up, to go down the single-flower-type track, and to put the bunch in a jar of water so she or he doesn't have to fuss around for a vase when you arrive.

Bouquets with too many elements head towards crappy-mixed-bunch territory very fast. If a CMB is what your friend is after, they most likely would have picked one up at the supermarket when they were getting bits and pieces for dinner. At the other end of the spectrum is the bridal bouquet vibe, an effect you can also end up with when you're playing with lots of different flowers. Probably a bit much for a Wednesday night dinner with your friend.

Another benefit of a bunch of a single type of flower is the intense focus it creates on that flower. The recipient has no choice but to drink in the beauty of, say, a fragrant bunch of spring sweet peas.

And the power of the emotions this singular focus can stir should not be underestimated.

English garden writer Anna Pavord, herself a passionate gardener, has spoken about her time in hospital when she was sick with cancer. Every day her husband would bring in a fresh bunch of sweet peas from their garden. When she stopped taking morphine, which made her wretch violently, Anna would concentrate on the scent of the sweet peas to get her through. She said the rich scent not only helped to pull her up out of her body, but also reminded her what there was to live for.

I'll never think of sweet peas in the same way again. What power such delicate little flowers can hold.

A simple bunch of sweet peas in a jar, including their lovely tendril bits, make a wonderful, fragrant springtime gift.

Bunches of vibrant dahlias in summer (above) and fragrant sweet peas in spring (right) are wonderful to use in flower gifts for a friend.

THE FLOWERS

Pick or buy a generous amount of the same flower, in the same or similar colours. My favourites in spring are sweet peas, flannel flowers, lilacs, mock orange, Iceland poppies and bundles of spring blossoms. In summer, how could you go past David Austin roses – although they are expensive. (Carnations, believe it or not, are a very good substitute. The double bloom cultivars like Chabaud La France are particularly beautiful, and fragrant.) And then there are hydrangeas, stripped of their green leaves and bunched at different heights into a cloud, or spilling, fragrant bunches of herbs like basil and nasturtiums. After a few days in water, the hydrangeas will start to dry out beautifully, while the nasturtiums will grow little roots and can be planted out in the garden. Or they can become part of dinner.

In autumn, there are anemones and dahlias and roses too, as well as bunches of cotton that will last well into winter – and for years beyond. In winter there's wattle, magnolias, camellias, dried, leggy hydrangeas, and dried honesty seed pods on their stems – somehow silver and gold at the same time. In late winter, you can also force a bunch of spring blossom branches to bloom ahead of their time by sitting them in water inside for a couple of weeks.

And all year round there are silver-grey olive leaves, gum leaves (the lemon-scented ones are my absolute favourite), and fragrant bundles of rosemary and bay.

Tip: If you are dealing with notorious wilters (see page 214) like lilacs or philadelphus (mock orange) – and both would make delightful bunches because of their incredible fragrance – do as Constance Spry suggests in her book *How to Do the Flowers* and pick all of their leaves off so that the flowers will last longer.

THE VESSEL AND THE WATER

Dig out a jar from the cupboard. The best ones to use are glass ones with a clamp lid attached so that when the flowers are dead and gone, your friend has a reusable jar. I have a stash of 600 ml (20 oz) glass clamp-lid jars, bought from the local two-dollar shop for $2.50 each, in my pantry for this purpose.

Make sure the jar is clean. I know everyone says this, but it actually is important. Cut flowers wilt when the water evaporating through their petals, leaves and stems is not replaced at the same rate by water from the vessel they are sitting in. The flowers suck it up through thin, tubular vessels in their stems. Dirty water contains microbes and dirt particles that can clog these vessels and limit their uptake, thus causing the flowers to wilt. If you want to be really thorough, after washing your vessels you can also give them a scrub with a bit of bleach, before filling them with flower-friendly water (page 28).

PREPPING AND ARRANGING

When you've got your clean vase full of flower-friendly water, gently plop whatever flowers you've chosen onto a table. Remove any lower leaves that might sit below the waterline, then arrange the stems either directly in the jar or in your hand. The advantage of arranging the bunch in your hand is how easily you can play around with composition, raising and lowering each stem without having to trim anything as you work.

To arrange the flowers in your hand, pretend you're holding an imaginary tennis racquet in your non-dominant hand and thread the stems into your loosely gripped fingers. When you've finished, you just cut the stems with secateurs to make them level. When arranging, it can help to picture a higher side and a lower side, with the stems all coming out from a central spot in your hand at different depths and heights. That way you won't end up with a perfectly domed shape or a flat one.

When you are happy – and I would not suggest spending too long on this; you want joyous spontaneity rather than 21st-century flower school precision – tie the bunch where you would naturally want to hold it. Check for any remaining low-hanging leaves and remove them.

Cut the stems so that they are level, but not too short. You want them to be able to reach the water when you place the bunch in the jar.

If you want to wrap the flowers in tissue paper, cast your eyes over the suggestions on page 88. But by all means, stop now. A simple bouquet in a jar is hard to beat.

If you plan to leave the bunch at a friend's door rather than handing them over yourself, include a parchment card bearing their name in your biggest, best city-florist calligraphy.

TOP

Japanese anemones, with their lower leaves removed and their stems cut, bunched up and tied up with string, ready to be wrapped in cloudy white tissue paper.

BOTTOM

The finished bunch is placed in a jar filled with flower-friendly water (see page 28).

At this stage of its life, cotton does not need to sit in water, which makes it the perfect material to be bunched up and given to a friend. Not only does it look like something out of a Seussian dream, you also don't have to fuss about with a water-filled vessel to keep it looking its best.

CLOUDY WHITE TISSUE WRAPPING

FLOWERS, WHITE PAPER, TISSUE OR WAX PAPER, RIBBON OR STRING, TAPE

●

The only way to improve your flower bouquet as a gift is to wrap the bundle in a big, blousy cloud of white tissue paper, and then another layer of white, heavy wrapping paper, while still keeping its legs firmly grounded in a jar of water. If you don't have any tissue or wrapping paper at home, fear not: baking paper does a very fine job.

Get two sheets of white paper and place them on a table. The sheets I used are 40 by 55 cm (16 by 22 in) – the hydrangeas I was wrapping were quite big, and because I wanted the paper to be big too, I did not fold them. If you have sheets that are bigger, or an arrangement that is smaller, fold one sheet in half, off-centre, and then the other. Position the two folded sheets so they make an upside-down V, overlapping at the top and with the fold lines facing in.

Get two pieces of tissue paper (the sheets I used are 50 by 75 cm/20 by 30 in) and repeat the folding process, placing them on top of the white paper. My preference is food-grade tissue paper that is a little stiffer than the stock-standard stuff you will find at the newsagency. But don't sweat it.

Place the bouquet on top of the paper, right in the centre, with the stems sitting in the negative space between the two sides of the upside-down V. Use the paper sheets to make a collar around the flowers, then secure it with ribbon or string at the base. Use a small bit of sticky tape to secure the two sheets together at the front and the back.

Re-cut the stems and immediately place the bunch in the water-filled jar. (In theory, every time you take the stems out of water they need a recut. CSIRO actually advises you to cut them underwater so that no air bubbles get trapped in the stems, but I'll leave it up to you to decide how militant you want to be.)

Left: First, create an upside-down V with two sheets of white paper on a tabletop or other flat surface.
Right: Next, add the second layer: white tissue paper folded in half off-centre.

Left: Place the bunch of flowers on top of the paper layers, with the stems extending over the edge of the upside-down V.
Right: Trim the stems, wrap the paper around the bunch, making the two sides overlap, and tie it off with string.

Your bunch is now ready to be put in a jar of water and given to your friend.

Top: Cut a hole in a shoebox large enough to fit your jar.

Bottom: Place your jar into the box and rest your construction in the footwell of your car to keep your flowers steady during transport.

Right: Alternatively, choose a jar that fits in one of your car's cup holders.

TRANSPORTING THE VASE

SHOEBOX OR SIMILAR, MARKER, SMALL SERRATED KNIFE

●

Though I was open to advice about cleaning jars and preparing water, it was not until sometime later that I accepted that I'd better work out how to stop all of my extra effort from tipping over in the car while I drove to my friend's house. Soggy sheets of tissue paper do not resemble clouds in the slightest. There's no coming back from that.

I have come up with a couple of solutions. You can always have a friend hold them for you, but if you're on your own, choose a jar that fits into your car's cup holder. It places certain limitations on the size of your bouquet, but otherwise is a very good transportation method. A bit of car garnish for the journey too.

Otherwise, invert a shoebox or similar, as long as it is no deeper than the jar is high, and cut a hole in the centre of the base the same size as the bottom of your chosen vessel. It's very easy. Just put the jar on top of the box, trace around it and saw out the circle with a small serrated knife. The flowers go in the jar, the inverted box goes in the footwell or on the passenger seat of the car, and the jar slots into the box. They all sit happily as you take on the bends to your friend's house without reservation.

SUPERMARKET FLOWERS

●

In short, I don't like them. Especially the hothouse commercial roses that smell precisely of nothing, whose scent has been sacrificed for shelf life. For a flower like the rose, whose identity is so tied up with its rich fragrance, the hothouse variety is especially disappointing. The scentless, perfectly straight, thornless bunches you find under the neon lights are the floral equivalent of the battery hen, produced with profit and efficiency in mind rather than pleasure or fragrance.

I do not begrudge the flower farmers for trying to make a buck as best they can, or the supermarket owners for wanting to stock products with decent shelf lives, but as a consumer I want to show there is a demand for natural roses. If I had the choice of buying one fragrant, flopsy rose over a dozen tall-stem scentless ones for the same amount of money, I'd buy the former. Hands down.

But I do understand that sometimes supermarket flowers are all you can get. And with a bit of thought, you can help return a sense of romance and pleasure to them. They are still, after all, natural. They were actually part of a living plant. They have petals and stamens and water-sucking vessels in their stems. Not all their natural magic can be bred out.

It is hard to imagine when you're faced with a stand of bought flowers – some of them actually dyed blue and wrapped in hideously patterned cellophane – but they can look joyful at home on your sideboard (though perhaps not the blue ones). Gerberas can look lovely in a vase, as can baby's breath. Especially baby's breath. Don't discriminate by type; it is more helpful to choose by colour. Keep it simple.

The addition of foraged flowers and foliage greatly enhances the appearance of supermarket-bought flowers. Here, I added peppercorns from a tree behind my local butcher shop.

The first thing you should do when you get your supermarket flowers home is to liberate them from their terrible wrapping, remove the lower leaves, recut the stems and place them in fresh water.

CHOOSING THE FLOWERS

Instead of buying pre-made bouquets, try to find a bunch or bunches of the same flower. It is much easier to work with a bunch of flowers of the same variety than many different flowers. Plus, straight bunches are cheaper. I don't see why you'd want to pay for the labour involved with the arranging when the arranging is no good in the first place.

Buy two, three, or even four bunches of the same flower. If you can't have fragrance, you may as well go for abundance. Take them home and immediately unwrap them from the garbage they've been swaddled in. Strip off most of their leaves, especially any soggy ones, and nine times out of ten you will need to throw any foliage 'filler' from the arrangement straight into the compost. Recut stems on the diagonal and let them sit in a bucket of fresh water while you dig out some jars, vases or jugs.

CREATING ARRANGEMENTS

Arrange the flowers in different jars, at different heights, in clusters down the middle of a table. Don't be scared to snip off a decent amount of some stems, and remember to cut them at different lengths. Garden flowers look great just plonked in a vase because of their natural irregularity, but the supermarket kind need some irregularity inserted into them. Get out those snippers.

Arrange a tableau of different vessels at various depths on a sideboard or, in my case in the summer, the wood-burning stove nook. It looks lovely when the flowers form a river flowing from left to right, up and down. Forget the rounded bouquet concept. Different heights, different depths, different vessels: that is what you need.

It also helps to add some natural bits and pieces from the garden or your morning walk, especially if they are a little dried out or woody. Some of these dirtier colours can tone down the sickly sweetness that is so common in supermarket bunches.

The appearance of supermarket flowers will be greatly enhanced by the addition of some garden-grown elements. Here, I have added pink peppercorns (from the *Schinus molle* pepper trees that grow behind my local butcher) to a mix of supermarket roses, gerberas and dahlias, along with some dried hydrangea heads that had been lurking on my dresser shelves for some months, and a few stems of chocolate Queen Anne's lace from the local florist.

RESCUING SUPERMARKET ROSES

Priggish supermarket roses can be significantly loosened up by blowing directly onto the tight flower heads, creating some space between the petals. You can also manually open them yourself. Starting from the outside layer, flip each petal out, one by one, to make them sit open. Imagine the wind flipping an umbrella inside out … that is what you are doing with the petals. You are the wind. It is tempting to try and open a heap of them at the same time, because most of us have better things to do with our lives, but this almost always ends badly. Instead, gently and steadily work your way around, opening each layer one petal at a time. When you reach the bud in the middle that is too tight to fold back, either leave it as it is or pluck it out entirely to reveal the stigmas – whatever your preference.

Et voila, you have a bunch of enormous, open, curvaceous roses. They may not smell like anything, but they will look lovely.

LEFT

The tight buds of the priggish supermarket rose can be significantly improved by manually inverting the closed petals, folding them out with your fingers one by one.

RIGHT

By cutting the stems at different lengths, you will eliminate the feeling of uniformity found in hothouse-grown roses.

04

AROUND THE TABLE

FOOD, WINE, FLOWERS

•

The very best dinner party advice comes from a French chef, Edouard de Pomiane. Along with sensibly recommending that dinner parties be made up of no more than eight people, he offers these sage words. There are three kinds of guests:

1. Those one is fond of.

2. Those with whom one is obliged to mix.

3. Those whom one detests.

For these three very different occasions, one would prepare, respectively: an excellent dinner, a banal meal, or nothing at all, since in the latter case one would buy something ready cooked.

Using this logic, which I enthusiastically do, the only dinner party guests you would have time to arrange flowers for are the ones whom you detest.

The people you love, although you might offer them a carefully prepared cassoulet and proper chocolate mousse for dessert, would be lucky to see a single flower on the table. This is the way it should be. After all, there is not much room left on a dinner table when it is full of food, wine glasses and the waving arms of those you love in animated conversation.

What matters more than fancy arrangements are the conversations shared and, of course, the food. Flowers can certainly enhance the atmosphere; they can convey a sense of care and love on behalf of the arranger, and of course they are beautiful, but they should in no way prevent people from seeing each other.

The following pages are filled with tablescape inspiration. Each lists an occasion and the flowers I used to complement it. They are suggestions only; you should feel free to take advantage of what's in season around you, and what is close at hand. And, above all, keep it simple.

ON THE TABLE

'Flowers on the table are delightful, but I think they are far more beautiful when naturally arranged (for which read "plonked"). Flower arrangers have a great deal to answer for.'

- NIGEL SLATER IN *REAL FAST FOOD*

The most important thing to keep in mind when planning flowers for a table is that the flowers are not the most important thing on that table.

I would go further and advise you to avoid arrangements entirely and, as Nigel says, plonk a few roses in a few small low vases. Single stems in tiny vases work very well, as do herbs.

If you are going to ignore this advice and place something more substantial in the middle of the table, make sure it is low enough for the people sitting at the table to talk over. A good rule of thumb is to place your elbow on the table, make a fist, straighten your forearm perpendicular to the table, and then make sure the flowers and foliage don't go any higher than your fist.

In terms of table real estate, flowers take second place to food. If there are to be shared plates in the middle of the table, make sure there is room for them. Don't let your flower-arranging ego lead you into making ridiculous decisions. The purpose of a lunch or dinner is for people to eat and socialise. Not to be isolated from the food or company by flowers, no matter how lovely they are.

Avoid putting sneezy things on the table if you are eating inside. As much as I love wattle, it sets my nose right off and is no good when I am trying to eat and/or talk and/or listen. I've heard you can hairspray wattle to trap the pollen, but do you really want to be the type of person who hairsprays wattle?

And don't underestimate the delightful surprise a bunch a fragrant flowers by the kitchen sink, or on a table near the front door, can bring. There may not be much room on the table, but there are plenty of opportunities for occasions of joy elsewhere.

A KITCHEN SUPPER

CLEMATIS, JAPANESE ANEMONE (FLOWERS AND LEAVES), PENSTEMON, ROSES, THISTLES

●

'Apart from the divinest colour of all the flowers that rejoice in our Northern air, infinite loveliness of form in bloom, branch, and tendril, there is the precious quality of a long season of bloom, which should endear them to all. Many well-loved flowers pass away like the clouds. Lilac time is too short; but there is no such sharp limit to the days of the Virgin's Bower.'

WILLIAM ROBINSON, *THE VIRGIN'S BOWER* (1913),
A 38-PAGE BOOK ON CLEMATIS

I adore the clematis. What other flower head can be so large, yet so delicate? The dahlia is frumpy by comparison; even the rose is a bit clunky. The clematis works particularly well on the table too. Its delicate, floaty nature results in minimal obstruction between talking heads. The clematis can gracefully spill over a vase and hover, face up, just above the table with gestural tendrils curling up and around. It is the loveliest thing to look down and see it staring up at you. And, as William Robinson suggests, the flowering season for clematis is long. For a good part of the year you can find at least one or two varieties flowering.

It's hard to beat a few small glass jars full of simple garden pickings and stems of clematis down the middle of the table. If your clematis cuttings come from a garden, be sure to leave on some of the woody stems – it will make them last longer.

A SPRING LUNCH

TWIGS COVERED IN LICHEN, JASMINE, OLIVE BRANCHES, GARDEN ROSES

Lichen-covered twigs, scattered in little piles down the length of a white linen-clad table, is a very pleasing sight. And it will take you about two minutes to put together. There are no vases to worry about; no obscuring of faces. And if you need to put something down the middle of the table – a water jug or a platter – you can easily make a little clearing among the twigs or plonk the platter straight on top of them.

In winter, I collect a few baskets of lichen-covered sticks and stack them in a pile in the shed. They sit there happily for months and months, ready to be called into action at the drop of a hat.

I think it works best when you crosshatch them down the middle of the table, but not too thickly – you are after a delicate, textural addition. As you arrange from above, imagine small, irregular, undulating waves of lichen twigs: little ups and downs.

If you can get your mitts on some delicate, fragrant flowering vines, like the white jasmine I used here, thread some lengths of it through the twigs. A couple of jugs of herbs or olive leaves one-third and two-thirds of the way down the table create some height variation on a very long table, but are not at all necessary.

If you have enough of the vine left over, fill a teapot with a trailing arrangement to bring a bit of fragrant love to the entranceway or the bathroom. A generous bunch of anything fragrant – perhaps a profusion of garden roses – above the kitchen sink can bring a great deal of joy to the chef (you), who is no doubt also the hostess, the waitress, the cleaner and the chief conversationalist.

A FRIDAY SUMMER'S EVE GATHERING

DAHLIAS, ROADSIDE FENNEL, BLACKBERRIES, GUM LEAVES, HEMLOCK*

●

Friday evenings are a sacred affair at home. We have dinner with the neighbours –
the same neighbours. We tell each other versions of the same stories while the kids run
around like maniacs, the same way they do every week. We plonk food and booze on
the table and everyone helps themselves. We take our plates outside if it's a pleasant
evening, or huddle by the fire in the kitchen if it is cool. There is something about this
repetition with my family, and the people who have come to feel like family, that
I find extremely comforting.

Most Fridays I can't be bothered to do anything fabulous with flowers, but when
I can summon the energy I am so glad I did. A room full of people I love; a table laden with
whatever shared dishes we've cooked; kids crawling underneath, brandishing makeshift
swords; the sound of dress-ups and plastic, clicky-clacky high heels coming from the
verandah, all surrounded by bikes and scooters and bundles of whatever is growing on
the side of the road or in the garden. It's more than I could ever want in this life.

*I thought I was picking Queen Anne's lace, another tall, white-flowering umbelliferous
roadside flower. That is what I should have been picking, and what I would suggest
you pick. Instead, I picked a very large bundle of poison hemlock, which is, as its name
indicates, poisonous. It's the stuff Socrates drank as he executed his own death sentence.
I have since learnt to differentiate the two: Queen Anne's lace (or wild carrot) has hairy
stalks and smells good, whereas hemlock has smooth, hollow stalks, sometimes with
purple splotches, and stinks. May this help you when you are in a roadside ditch, secateurs
in one hand and a bunch of weeds in the other.

Large bundles of hemlock (I mistook it for Queen Anne's lace), fennel and gum leaves, in various stages of decay, make the most beautiful background for dinner and Aperol spritzes in the shed.

A SUMMER DINNER

CREPE MYRTLE, FIG LEAVES, COSMOS, OLIVE SPRIGS, GUM BRANCHES,
BASIL, GARDEN ROSES

The barbecue is on and the champagne is in the fridge. The ice trays are empty –
how do I always forget to refill the damn things – and people are on their way over
for a dinner that would have been outside if the flies weren't so bad.

Instead we will eat in the kitchen, with all the fly-screened windows wide open.
I've made a grape and rosemary focaccia to nibble on with the aperitifs. We'll then
have grilled chicken with tomatoes, olives and basil for dinner, and honey-roasted
figs and cream for dessert.

I've got a couple of minutes up my sleeve, so I pull out my favourite little vases and
snake them down the middle of the table, plopping them in among some of the
grapes and summer fruit I didn't use while making the meal.

I duck outside and snip whatever I see – a few roses, some basil, some fig leaves,
a few cosmos – and plop the little sprigs into each vase, making sure none of
them sit above seated chin height. (Can I make a point here that I do not live at
Sissinghurst. Ducking out to pick a few things may sound like the privilege of
someone like Vita Sackville-West, but really, it's only a matter of planting a couple
of bare-rooted roses in winter, sewing a few seeds in spring, and managing to
not kill the stumpy fig tree near the kitchen door, which I want to do each winter
because it is an awful, miserable thing to look at.)

It's not a practical thing to do from a washing-up perspective, but I then put a
bucket in one half of the kitchen sink, fill it with water, and stuff the branch of
a hot pink crepe myrtle in it, along with some errant olive branches and dried
gum branches that fell from their tree. In front, I add a level of fragrant roses and
their foliage. It feels festive and joyful, which is how I feel tonight. The dirty dishes
will just have to be piled on the floor.

AN AUTUMN DINNER
IN THE PADDOCK

CHESTNUT BRANCHES, PUMPKINS, AN IRON GARDEN OBELISK

●

I do love the look of a singular long table stretching out through a paddock or on the lawn, but you are rather stuck with your immediate table neighbours. This can be a good thing or a bad one. A U-shaped configuration for gatherings of 20-plus guests gives everyone more options for who to strike up conversation with. It can feel miraculously less claustrophobic *and* more intimate, especially under the canopy of a tree, real or makeshift.

Steel or iron garden obelisk structures make building a makeshift tree a cinch. Secure the obelisk on the ground in the middle of the U-shaped table arrangement with tent pegs or stakes. Angle two large branches into the top third of the obelisk so that they are counterbalanced. (Find a friend to steady the structure while you add in the first few branches.) Continue adding branches – I have used chestnut branches, but you can use anything you like – using the counterbalancing method until you are happy with your canopy. For added stability, weigh down the base of the obelisk with sandbags or the like and camouflage them with something seasonal. Here, I have used pumpkins.

A FANCY AUTUMN LUNCH
ON THE LAWN

AUTUMN HYDRANGEAS, JAPANESE ANEMONES, ROSES, GARDEN FOLIAGE

Here is proof that a flower table arrangement does not have to be complicated
to be lovely.

Create one low arrangement for the centre of the table using autumnal garden
bits and bobs. Here, I used a ceramic baking dish filled with water and balled-
up chicken wire secured with a grid of floral tape (see page 28). I then angled in
hydrangeas, anemones, roses and foliage, adding a few little piles of hydrangeas
(autumn hydrangeas will happily sit out of water for a while) and some candles
at intervals down the table. The gaps between the piles of hydrangeas left ample
room for shared platters.

One low arrangement of hydrangeas, roses and Japanese anemones sits at the centre of the long lunch table. Little clusters of hydrangeas are dotted either side of the central arrangement, allowing plenty of room in-between for the shared plates of roast chicken, salad and vegetables.

A PICNIC

QUEEN ANNE'S LACE, ROSES, PELARGONIUMS, DAHLIAS, FRUITING BRANCHES OR WHATEVER IS BLOSSOMING AROUND YOU

●

'Have a picnic at the slightest excuse.'

JAMES BEARD, *MENUS FOR ENTERTAINING* (1965)

Picnic is my favourite word in the English language (only after *miffed*), especially when used as a verb. To go picnicking. Doesn't it conjure up the happiest memories of Ratty and Mole feasting on cold chicken, cress sandwiches and ginger beer on the banks of the river in *The Wind in the Willows*? Australian picnics are not always as idyllic as their European counterparts from my childhood reading. You've got to contend with flies, sometimes snakes, and of course scratchy, dry grass. But even with these drawbacks, I think an afternoon spent picnicking under the shade of a tree, preferably near a running stream, is hard to beat.

Fill an old toolbox with cutlery and condiments and stack a few plates, cups, picnic blankets and pillows in a wicker basket. Bring a big thermos of cold water and a few bottles of even colder wine, along with some bread and cold cuts and a tart for dessert, and you have almost everything you need. Perhaps throw in the barbecue and some sausages if you feel so inclined.

I find picnicking is made much easier if you have at least one hard surface to act as a buffet table – either a trestle table or an old pallet will do the trick. And the only other thing I would suggest you bring is a jug or jar to act as a vase for some flowers for the buffet table. Ideally, you'd pick the flowers from the spot you are picnicking in: some wild Queen Anne's lace or dandelions. Otherwise, just bring a simple bunch of roses or pelargoniums (commonly known as geraniums), whatever is in season, and plonk them in the jug. If your buffet table has legs, it can also look lovely to place a pot of something flowering at the base of it. It softens the transition between the grass and the tabletop, creating a gentler look, as if the table has sprung up out of the meadow around it.

Above: A picnic buffet table with a simple jug of long-stemmed garden roses is a wonderful summer's sight.

Right: A small ceramic jug filled with white pelargoniums sits next to the chilled cassis cordial and iced coffee drink dispensers.

Above: An old toolbox makes a great container for napkins, cutlery, salt, pepper and condiments.
Below: What could be a more welcome sight than a day bed in the shade, piled with blankets and books, with a rusty bucket of roses at its feet?

A LITTLE WINTER LUNCH

DRIED HYDRANGEAS

●

Dried hydrangeas last forever, or near enough. I keep a little bundle of them in
a cupboard at home and pull them out when I am chasing something delicate
and feminine in the depths of winter.

To dry the hydrangeas, pick or buy a bunch in summer or autumn and place them
in a water-filled vase. Don't top up the water; just let them dry out naturally.
By the time the water has disappeared, you will have a bunch of dried hydrangeas
that can be left to sit in the vase forevermore, hung upside-down or stored in a
cupboard until you need them.

UP AND OVER

When it comes to flowers for a dinner party, a good way to avoid blocking people from seeing each other is to forget the table completely and take it all overhead. That is my favourite way to handle flowers for table gatherings of more than 12 people. For these larger parties, you are often dealing with narrow trestle tables that have been bought cheaply or hired, which means there is even less space for flowers than usual. So break out some chicken wire and take it up and over.

Which reminds me of a conversation I once had with my farmer father-in-law.

'Are you doing a bit of fencing?' he inquired as he opened the boot of my car to help me carry the groceries inside.

'No,' I said. 'They are for flowers.'

To which he replied – rather unkindly I thought: 'Dear God'. After all, some people keep golf clubs in their boot.

There is not much room for fruit and veg on top of the mobile flower installation kit I keep permanently in the boot: large rolls of chicken wire, saws, secateurs (blunter than they should ever be), fishing line, zip ties in all sizes (some black, others clear), black spray paint, an impossibly heavy urn, wire cutters, an axe and some large glass cylindrical vases, one of which has shattered into a million pieces that I can't quite bring myself to deal with – those sorts of things.

The single most useful bit of kit in this assemblage is the zip tie, otherwise known as the cable tie. I prefer 'zip' because that is the sweet sound it makes when you pull it tight with your teeth as you secure a rather heavy branch of autumn leaves, which you are only just managing to hold up with two shaking arms, near a very high beam that you can only reach by standing on your tippy-toes on the highest rung of a very tall ladder.

One day I will die doing this, when I make the tragic error of doing up the zip tie with its corrugated side facing out instead of in. Instead of the zippy sound of a successful fastening, there will be the silent, ratchet-less glide of the tie into and then out of itself, followed by the dual thuds of the heavy branch and me hitting the ground.

When organising the resulting funeral, someone will ask poor Ed, 'Would you like flowers for your wife's service, or is that too close to the bone?' And Ed, who for much of his married life has, with great dignity, endured enforced stops on the side of the road to cut bushels of weeds, and long car trips with itchy fennel poking him in the ear, will reply, stony-faced and resolute: 'There will be no more flowers'. He will remarry a bench wiper who makes everyone take their shoes off before coming inside and will force my daughters to wear fake flowers in their hair on their wedding days.

This is what runs through my head when I'm precariously dangling from a dodgy beam: *Is it bumpy side in, or bumpy side out? I can't remember.*

This kind of angst is not sustainable, so now I chant – in the vein of other puerile but helpful phrases like 'my life's motto is B-positive', which helps me remember my blood type – 'bump-side in for the win'. Or in full:

> *Smooth inside means fake-flower bride*
>
> *Bumps inside means me alive*
>
> *Bump-side in for the win*
>
> *Bump-side in for the win*

The roll of chicken wire, on the other hand, is much simpler, and therefore more lovely, than the ever-useful-but-it's-complicated zip tie. And if you are a one-woman team, it allows you to create big installations with minimal fuss.

Going up and over is really only something I do for a very special occasion or for someone else – as a paid job, or for a friend. If people are coming over to my house for dinner, I've got other priorities. Like cooking, vacuuming and wondering where I've put the flipping napkins.

CREATING AN OVERHEAD INSTALLATION

Chicken wire is pliable but firm, easy to transport and easy to rig up. There is no right or wrong side. It is strong and, unless observed up close, is more or less invisible. It can hold heavy things overhead. It allows for the construction of waves and firework bursts of branches and foliage. I love it unconditionally. In a situation where you are hanging things from overhead beams, it really is the most wonderful tool.

I buy rolls of 50 by 50 mm (2 by 2 in) hexagonal chicken wire – 1.2 m (4 ft) wide at a gauge of 1 or 0.9 mm (.04 in), either 10 or 30 m (30 or 100 ft) long and cut where necessary. Longer rolls are too heavy to schlep around and carry up ladders, so don't be tempted by the cheaper per-metre price.

A good rule of thumb is to keep overhead arrangements at least 1 m (3 ft) above the table so that seated guests can see each other, but I do love the occasional tendril or delicate branch of foliage dipping below to create an in-the-forest feeling. Play around with different heights and the different moods that come with each.

You can go down the path of botanical design studio Loose Leaf (look them and their monstera chandeliers up if you don't know them – their work is astounding), balling up 1 by 1 m (3 by 3 ft) pieces of chicken wire, hanging them from the beams at different heights and depths and then stuffing your foliage into them.

Or, if you have access to a room with overhead beams, you can go down the floating carpet path.

Unfurl the chicken wire as if you are rolling out a red carpet, to a length about as high as the beam is off the ground. Rustle up a ladder from which you can comfortably reach the beam. Climb the ladder with a pocket full of zip ties and the end of the unfurled chicken wire in one hand. Don't try to carry the entire roll up the ladder – leave the weight of it on the ground and just take the unfurled length up with you.

Secure the end of the chicken wire by wrapping it around the beam and zip-tying or wiring it in at least four spots, weaving the zip ties in and out of several hexagonal cells and around the entire beam.

Then move your ladder to the next beam. Haul up the roll of chicken wire and, leaving a generous swag between the first and second beams, nudge the roll over the top of the second beam and let it fall with a thud to the ground, holding the wire in place on top of the beam.

Shift your ladder to the third beam and repeat the process. If the beams are too close together, skip every second beam.

When you get to the last beam, adjust the swags of wire. To make them less dippy, pull the wire to make the roll shorter. To make the swags longer, do the opposite. When you are happy with the wave of them, cut the roll, wrap the new end around the last beam and secure it with zip ties in at least four places. Go back to the previous beams and whack in a few zip ties to keep the wave in place.

Now you are ready to insert autumn branches, bursts of tall fennel, gum leaves, cotton – anything that can handle being out of water for a day or two. Weave the stems of the branches over and under the hexagonal cells for extra stability. Thread the branches into central points at different angles and depths, securing them with zip ties where necessary. Angle in some branches from on top of the wave – some can actually rest horizontally on the stretch of chicken wire. Angle things into the wire from underneath the canopy too. If you have any doubts about the branches staying put, secure them with zip ties or wire.

For large rooms, unless you have lots of time and material, it is more effective to create firework explosions at different points along the chicken wire instead of trying to fill every square inch of it.

This old church was a dream. Not only did it have wonderfully textured walls, it also had very high ceilings and overhead beams. I hung a roll of chicken wire from them, letting the wire blanket hang in swags in-between the beams. Starting from the first beam, I built little explosions of autumn branches up and down the wire magic carpet. From the floor, it looked as though the ceiling was a wild wave of autumnal reds and yellows.

Left: Tall and light in weight, this branch – and branches like it – are exactly what you want to look for when you are building your overhead explosions. Steer clear of particularly heavy branches – they are a pain to work with and tend to distort the curved waves of the chicken wire magic carpet.

AN AUTUMN DINNER PARTY

COTTON BRANCHES, DRIED LEAVES, ZIP TIES

●

I really don't understand why people get bothered about leaves on the floor. Of all the things to clean up, they are the easiest and most pleasant. A quick sweep and everything is as good as new. Plus, the crunching sound of an autumn leaf underfoot takes me straight back to my childhood, throwing myself into the mounds of fallen leaves piled up on the footpath.

After cotton harvest in autumn, I like to zip tie some bunches of it to the overhead beam in my kitchen, undulating up and down and in and out. First, create ten or so bunches of cotton at ground level, securing each bunch together at the point where you would naturally want to hold it (much as you would when making a bouquet, see page 84) with a zip tie. Then shimmy up a ladder and tie each bunch to the beam with string or zip ties – some higher, some lower, some pointing diagonally left or right.

There the bunches of cotton will stay for several months, until I feel like a change.

Occasionally, a little ball of cotton will fall off but, just as with the leaves on the ground, a quick sweep will bring everything back into order.

A cloud of cotton overhead and a floor of crunchy leaves underfoot
make a delightful setting for an autumn lunch in the kitchen.

A SPRING BIRTHDAY PARTY

AUSTRALIAN MISTLETOE, OLD BOATING ROPE, ZIP TIES, FAIRY LIGHTS, JASMINE

If your venue has overhead beams, like here in my neighbour's magnificent shearing shed, you have won the floral installation lottery. It makes the mechanics of suspending foliage from the ceiling a breeze.

While you are at ground level, create several bunches of foliage – some longer than others, and enough to run above the length of the table. (Here, I made about ten bunches: some very short, some very long and others in-between.) Tie them off at the stems with zip ties.

Climb up a ladder and, one by one, tie each bunch to the beam with zip ties, string or wire, letting them hang upside down. Keep in mind an undulating river running above and, at times, just below seated head height. It helps to have a friend calling out 'higher', 'lower', and 'way too short' from the ground while you are up on the ladder.

I used bunches of Australian mistletoe, the semi-parasitic plant you often see hanging like chandeliers from gum trees. They have a wonderful weeping, tiered shape and work very well hanging overhead. Northern Hemisphere mistletoes work well too, although they are not quite so pendulous. Weeping willow branches bunched together create the same effect, or any foliage or vines with a trailing quality.

Hang an old, heavy fishing rope and lengths of fairy lights (warm white globes, please) in swags, bringing different textures and layers to the installation's wave shape.

Little added bonuses of sweet-smelling jasmine in the kitchen and bathroom will create a wonderful perfume and provide a boost for the chef.

Above: These naturally pendulous branches work exceptionally well above this table in a shed.
The mistletoe has the added advantage of lasting incredibly well out of water.
Left: A jar of jasmine on the mantle above the stove scents the nearby kitchen.

A SUMMER DINNER PARTY IN A HALL

GUM, WATTLE, SMOKEBUSH, ROSEMARY, APPLE BRANCHES, WELDMESH, OLD WOODEN LADDERS, ZIP TIES, EYE SCREWS, DRILL, CHAIN OR TENSION WIRE

You are standing in a nondescript, empty hall. You've volunteered to do the flowers for a long-table dinner for 80 people. You have a budget of $0. There are no overhead beams. But you *do* have a piece of weldmesh in the back of the ute and a friend with a couple of ladders, a drill and a large rosemary hedge at his house. And that is just about everything you need to make a ceiling thick and dripping with gorgeous summer foliage.

An installation like this one immediately creates a sense of intimacy in a large, almost cavernous space.

BUILD THE HANGING STRUCTURE

We drilled seven eye screws into the ceiling (where there was a beam behind, obviously) in two rows down the length of the table: 14 screws in total. And then with chains – some tension wire would have been more discreet, but when you have a nonexistent budget you have to work with what you've got – we suspended the weldmesh so that it would hang above, and parallel to, the centre of the table. Then, leaving a gap of at least a metre on either side, we suspended two old wooden ladders (approximately 2 by 1 m/6.5 by 3 ft) on either side of it. The weldmesh is ugly, so you want to cover it completely with branches, but the wooden ladders have a lovely patina and so don't need to be completely obscured.

CREATE YOUR ARRANGEMENT

When your structure is in place, go and beg, borrow or steal whatever branches, foliage or flowers you can. I used a mix of gum, wattle, smokebush, rosemary and roadside apple branches. All but the apple leaves can stand being out of water very well. The apple leaves will wilt a little, but because these branches were laden with apples they still looked beautiful.

While you are at ground level, bundle up the foliage into separate bunches of varying sizes and lengths, tying them with zip ties or string. Then, one by one, attach the bunches to the weldmesh by zip-tying the stems to the metal grid. You are aiming to create a wide chandelier shape. Start by fixing the longest branches into the centre of the weldmesh grid, and then gradually angle in shorter bunches as you work your way outwards. Rather than having the branches hang straight down, try to angle them in to create a three-dimensional chandelier shape.

Hide the top of the weldmesh with some light foliage. Then attach a few branches to the hanging ladders with zip ties or string, allowing the weldmesh chandelier to taper off on either side with some airier foliage.

The muted elegance of dried honesty seed pods.

TWO DINNER PARTIES IN A BARN

VERSION 1: STEMS OF HONESTY SEED PODS, METAL RIM, SMALL CHAIN, WIRE, STRING
VERSION 2: GRASS SODS, ROSES, LINDEN, PRUNUS, OAK BRANCHES, ZIP TIES

●

I really love the challenge of finding myself in unknown territory and creating an installation using only what's lying around. Here, in this wonderful old barn, there were no overhead beams that I could loop a rope around or tie some wire to. But there were some very long sticks, and crooks in which they could sit where the support joists met the main vertical beams. And so, without any drilling, sawing or anything laborious, a usable overhead beam and two very different floral scenes were born.

VERSION 1: MUTED ELEGANCE

Take a metal rim (I found one loose on one of the old wine barrels in the barn) and suspend it from the makeshift overhead beam with a small chain. Level it up with some thin wire, then attach some upside-down stems of dried honesty seed pods (which were very conveniently growing in the garden). The honesty is so light that all you have to do is tie a few stems to pieces of string, and attach them close to the beam. Let them hang down and outwards, over the rim, creating a three-dimensional cone.

If you don't have a metal rim, anything circular will do: a hula hoop, a wreath made of grapevines (page 148) or a few bendy saplings. Or you could, on ground level, create a wide bunch of the honesty, tie it off and then suspend it over the table upside-down.

VERSION 2: COLOURFUL AND FRAGRANT

Starting at the base of a vertical beam, create a little meadow explosion that looks as if it is growing out of the ground. Do this by carting in some grass sods, dug out with the soil still attached to the roots. Once you've created a pile of grassy dirt, jam in other, taller roadside weeds so that they look as if they are growing up and around the beam. If your dirt has low clay content and is not able to hold the stems in place, add some balls of chicken wire – or even the dreaded floral foam – and obscure it with some grass.

When you are happy with your mini meadow, the size of which will depend on how much space you have (mine was about 80 by 80 cm/31 by 31 in, nestled around the vertical beam), zip-tie branches and stems of whatever is growing nearby to the beam. I used roses and linden, prunus and oak branches so that they wind their way up and over the horizontal beam. They were happy enough out of water for the night. I would not, however, put this together the day before the event, as the fresh green growth will wilt.

Zip-tie more foliage to the horizontal beam, letting any particularly fragrant or beautiful blooms droop down so they can be enjoyed.

A more colourful and fragrant take on the barn. Here, an explosion of grass, roadside weeds and thistles surrounds the base of the beam, while prunus and linden branches snake their way up and overhead, punctuated by long stems of fragrant garden roses.

AN AUTUMN DINNER PARTY

GUM, WATTLE, ORANGE BRANCHES, POTTED PRICKLY PEARS, WOODEN ARBOUR (BRANCHES, ELECTRIC SAW, PLYWOOD, DRILL, SCREWS), ZIP TIES

If you have tables that you can drill into and that look good without a tablecloth, your scope for overhead structures grows significantly larger. This dinner party was to be held outside; there were no large trees or pergola structures that I could leech off for my installation. So with the help of a builder friend and the very obliging owner of some plywood trestle tables, we built our own. I say 'builder friend' to give credit where credit is due, rather than to imply that you need to be a builder to do this. If you can use an electric saw and a drill – which most of us can – you can make this.

CONSTRUCT YOUR ARBOUR

Find two branches that are slender, but strong – about 5 to 7 cm (2 to 3 in) in diameter – with natural Y-shaped crooks. With an electric saw, cut the branches so that their crooks stand at about the same height and at least 1 m (3 ft) above the tabletop. Trim the ends of the Ys so that they are level. Then find another slender branch – crookless this time – that is more or less straight, and long enough to rest in between the Ys and parallel to the tabletop.

Cut two square pieces of plywood – for branches that are about 5 cm (2 in) in diameter, you'll want a plywood base of approximately 15 by 15 cm (6 by 6 in). Using a drill, screw them into the flat base of your Y branches to create a little base for them to stand on, which will then be screwed into the table. You could make the bases much bigger and perhaps bypass the need to screw the arbour into the table, but then the bases could get in the way of plates and cups, and it would be so horrific if the arbour were to fall over that I would almost always recommend screwing it down. If you have tables that cannot be screwed into, pick a different method of going up and over.

When it's in place, nestle the remaining branch lengthwise between the two Y branches.

CREATE YOUR ARRANGEMENT

Add foliage to your structure (with zip ties, of course). I used gum, wattle and orange branches, but any foliage, particularly if it is light and trailing, would be lovely. Because the arbour itself is lovely, you don't need to fully obscure it. Just add in some foliage that goes up and down on both sides of the beam.

I really love seeing the natural wood of the branch structure; it's as if these orange-laden trees are growing up and out of the table. Plus it leaves plenty of room for food and drinks on the tabletop. I used some potted-up prickly pears from the paddock to disguise the plywood bases. Grass sods or small arrangements would do the trick too.

A WINTER LUNCH
WATTLE (THAT'S IT)

●

Just as the semi-parasitic mistletoe uses its host tree as a structure over which to sprawl, so too can you use winter-dormant arbours covered in deciduous vines as your installation structure. No chicken wire, zip ties or any sort of drilling required.

Here is a wisteria-clad arbour, the leaves and racemes of the warmer months long gone: the perfect structure under which to set up a table for a winter lunch. Find something that flowers in winter – I've used the glorious branches of wattle, or mimosa, as it is more kindly known in the Northern Hemisphere – and thread it into the naked vines.

A SUB ROSA LUNCH

ROSES, GRAPEVINE CUTTINGS, FISHING LINE, A CEILING HOOK

The ancient Romans would paint roses – the emblem of the god of secrecy – on the ceilings of banquet rooms to cast a veil of confidentiality over what was said by those around the table. And because of all the wine served at those feasts, I imagine what was said was pretty juicy.

In the Middle Ages, a single rose would hang from the ceiling over council chamber meetings as a call for discretion, giving the speakers the freedom to speak candidly. And it is because of these customs that, today, we have decorative ceiling roses around our light fixtures. So why not make a rose wreath to hang above your table the next time your intimates come over for a bite and a gossip?

FORAGE FOR A BASE RING

First up, you need to create the base ring for your wreath. You can go natural or find something that is already round, like your child's hula hoop.

For a natural base, it is hard to beat grapevine cuttings. It also helps that my neighbour has a very vigorous ornamental vine that requires annual pruning after it has lost its leaves. (I make up a heap of wreaths of different sizes with the just-pruned vines and let them sit in the shed until I need them. As the vines age, they dry and become brittle and it is hard to shape them, although you can soak them in the bathtub to inject a bit of flexibility back into them.) I love the look of little squiggly bits that come off the vine. They act like natural fasteners, making it very easy to work with. You just need a couple of lengths of grapevine.

Hold one end in your non-dominant hand, and with your dominant hand, grasp about two-thirds of the way up its length. Bring your hands together to make a circle, clasp the vines where they overlap, and use your dominant hand to tuck any leftover length in and around the circle. It should be quite secure, thanks to the squiggly bits. Weave another length of vine in and around the existing circle to shore it up. If you are worried about it staying together, tie it off with string.

CREATE YOUR ROSE WREATH

Weave some rose stems into your wreath, letting some flower heads dangle down and others up. The roses will happily sit out of water for a day. I also don't mind the more withered look the roses take on when their leaves wilt and the petals dry out. If that bothers you, make the wreath the day of, or before, the lunch.

Fasten a ceiling hook into the ceiling above the table. Tie a length of fishing line to one side of the wreath, then up through the ceiling hook and down to the other side of the wreath. The fishing line look is particularly pleasing when you are suspending relatively light structures like this one because it creates the illusion of the wreath floating above the table.

05

SPECIAL OCCASIONS

TWO WEDDINGS
AND A FUNERAL

•

THERE'S A CHARMING CUSTOM IN AUSTRALIAN RURAL towns whereby local women voluntarily do the flowers for their friends' weddings and funerals. Out of love, and perhaps out of necessity. In many of these towns there's either no florist at all or one whose preference is to work with plastic flowers – carnations at a stretch.

So local women step in, offering up their time and the flowers from their gardens, because they want to help. Because they value their community and because they care. They want the day to be beautiful for the bride, who they may or may not know very well. Using a combination of creative talent, kind hearts and green thumbs, these women act as the unpaid resident florists. There is a need, and they fill it.

I keep saying women, sorry. There must be some men out there who do the flowers as a community service, but I have yet to see one in action. They seem to be tied up with paid work or saving up their volunteering time for jobs of the shifting-tables variety.

I was brought up in Sydney suburbia in the '80s, where the needs of the individual had all but squashed collectivism. Suburban plots that used to be more garden than house became more house than garden. People got electric openers for their front gates. A friend's mother, who ran a weekend roadside flower stall, was shut down by council because it wasn't safe – something to do with parked cars on the road.

I am not sure whether it was in keeping with the times or with my mum and dad's ideas, but I was indoctrinated with the belief that if you needed something, you paid someone to do it. Don't impose yourself on friends or neighbours. Don't bother anyone outside of your immediate family with requests for help. Learn to look after yourself, and work hard to earn money so that you can.

So you can imagine how, as an adult, I find it almost inconceivable to not only see these women putting aside time to help others so freely, but also – especially – to see those getting married, or the families organising a funeral, actually accepting that offer.

It speaks of generosity, care and community. And even though you can't capture the value of an interaction like this in monetary terms, the value is real. We all know it. To love and be loved is an elemental human desire. So often we get in the way of fulfilling this desire by paying strangers to help us instead of opening up to the people around us.

Through their actions, these volunteer florists are saying 'I see you celebrating', or 'I see you hurting, and I am here to help'. And by accepting this help, their friends are replying without words, 'I am worthy of your love. I am part of this community. Thank you'.

To me, this is a revolutionary way of interacting with your fellow man. It's certainly different to paying someone to do it and getting all snarky if the boutonnieres wilt.

Think of all the stories the volunteer florists get from this work. Think of what these women have seen and done, thanks to their efforts. They've seen grooms hiding in cool rooms on cruelly hot days while the bride, who they've known since birth, is sweating foundation and shaking with nerves, white-knuckling her bouquet. They've tastefully repurposed flowers from an Easter wedding for an unexpected funeral the next day, referring to the flowers as 'twice blessed'. They've pulled off birdcage-themed weddings. They've made giant flowers out of cardboard and crepe paper for engagement parties during droughts when the gardens were bare.

They can tell if a marriage is destined to flourish (the groom is very helpful with preparations in the days leading up to the wedding, stacking, carting and then unstacking chairs, stringing up lights and following instructions) from one that probably won't last (the groom spends the days before the wedding drinking booze by the pool while the mother-in-law and friends set everything up).

In the days before a local wedding, the flower ladies dust off their collection of urns, home-welded flower stands and tremendously heavy, large glass battery jars stuffed with ancient blobs of floral foam, all collected over the course of decades. They will strip their gardens of all their flowers and lug everything out to the wedding venue via multiple car trips. Then they will work together to deck out the woolshed or marquee or backyard and make it as fabulous as possible, consuming lots of cups of tea and sandwiches that someone has brought along or offered to make out of the kindness of their heart. Often there is a boss (well, there may be several, but each event can only really have one), and the boss has a distinctive style. 'You can go to a funeral and know that

Penny has done the flowers,' said a friend of mine from a town nearby.

The flowers and foliage they use are, by default, local to the area and specific to that time of year, which has a rather modern ring to it.

I've been communicating with women who have some experience in this department. One lady recounted how when her grandmother died, her family gathered flowers and foliage from their nearby gardens and brought it all in for her to arrange for the funeral: 'Every year on the anniversary of Nan's funeral, the same flowers are blooming in their gardens and it's really special'.

Another woman was worried about what she and her family would do for their Mum's memorial service, held in a friend's beautiful country garden: 'We needn't have worried. Those special country women arrived like magic, with no fuss and a huge arrangement in a massive urn'.

And from another lady, who was married in a small town: 'My wedding bouquet was all local roses, picked over three or four days from the local gardens in town and kept fresh in the cool room of the kitchen in the *hospital* (my emphasis, not hers). The fragrance was so heady and glorious ... some of the rose bushes were 60 years old ... and the next day I placed the bouquet on my father's grave. He had died seven years earlier'.

Because I'm now a country girl, I thought it would be interesting to put my suburban each-to-their-own attitude on ice and give this way of life a try. So when a friend asked if I would help her with the flowers for her wedding in a woolshed on a cattle farm, I quickly said yes. She had a budget of $800, which we used to buy buckets of peonies from a farm in the next town over. The rest of the flowers I could get from her mother-in-law's friend Jules down the road.

Off I went to Jules's garden, past fields of cows and sheep and poplar trees, expecting it would be a few garden beds around a house on a farm at the end of a dirt road. But I had significantly underestimated the garden. It was magnificent, enormous. And there, in the middle of it all, was Jules, who created this paradise with her husband over the course of decades, one garden bed at a time. She welcomed me, my four-wheel drive and my trailer, and said I could pick whatever I wanted.

'Even this dogwood?' I asked, not believing her.

'Yes, of course. And let me get you a ladder so you can get those good roses too.'

While some people would have guarded such a glorious garden, Jules wanted nothing more than to share it. Even at the end of a rose-picking frenzy, as I was wiping the sweat from my brow and starting to head for the water buckets, Jules was insistent I pick more, yelling from a distant garden bed where she was picking something else for me, 'Get some more. You haven't got enough'.

So I dutifully put my head back down and kept on snipping.

What follows are some suggestions for what to do if you get the chance to do the flowers for a friend, whether it be for a big wedding, a small wedding or a funeral. You can do it, even if you are not a professional florist.

This chapter will walk you through events I did the flowers for, explaining what I used and how I went about arranging them, with the hope that they will act as a useful guide for your own adventures in flower arranging. My advice is rambling and suggestive. Jules, however, was very definite with hers: 'Start early'.

Above: The bride, her mother and two bridesmaids hard at work, removing leaves from the branches of dogwood.
Right: I still cannot believe Jules let me cut these glorious dogwood branches from her garden.

ON BOUQUETS

In ancient Greek and Roman times, brides typically did not carry a bouquet of flowers. They wore wreaths on their heads, as did the grooms, and often the whole wedding party. What a wonderful sight that would have been. The Roman *corona nuptialis* – the bridal wreath – was made of flowers, often verbena. It was usually picked by the bride herself, a fact I find very pleasing.

Over the ages, wreaths have been joined by bouquets. In 1840, Queen Victoria wore a wreath of orange blossoms instead of a tiara and carried a small bouquet of snowdrops, which were her beloved Albert's favourite flower. (To me, this is the epitome of what a bouquet should be. Sentimental and simple.) Now wreaths are called flower crowns, and for the most part are a bonus add-on to the bouquet, which tends to play the starring role.

And what a role they play. Poor Lady Di, carrying that enormous cascading three-kilogram bouquet down the aisle, with her dress's eight-metre train behind her and a doomed marriage ahead.

I think Grace Kelly, the princess of Monaco, is a better role model in the wedding bouquet department. She carried a small clutch of lily-of-the-valley stems. Delicate, fragrant and simple. What could be more lovely?

An all-white autumnal bouquet of pelargoniums, iceberg roses, dahlias, daisies and flowering potato vine.

MAKING A BOUQUET

Making a bridal bouquet is very similar to crafting a bunch of flowers to take to a friend (page 83). For the latter, I suggest sticking to one type of flower, but here you can get a bit more adventurous (although, like Grace Kelly's lily-of-the-valley bouquet, the one type of flower arrangement is pretty hard to beat).

Gather whatever flowers you've chosen – either one type or a combination of flowers and foliage, some full, some delicate, some trailing – and remove any lower leaves. Loosely wrap the fingers of your non-dominant hand around an imaginary broom handle, then begin threading the flowers into the circle of your hand. The advantage of arranging the bunch in your hand is that you can easily play around with composition by raising and lowering each stem as you go. It also helps that you can hold it in front of your waist, just as the bride would. Stand in front of a mirror so you can get the front view as well as the top.

When arranging, it can help to picture the bouquet having a high side and a low side: a relatively wide arrangement with different depths and heights. You don't want a perfectly domed shape or a flat one, but rather an undulating river.

Start with a few of your biggest flowers. Be careful not to cross the stems over each other as you thread them in. You want the stems to sit parallel, either in line or on top of the existing stem line. Crossed stems can break under the pressure of holding the bouquet, particularly if the bride is nervous.

Pepper in some of the lighter elements, then work in another group of flowers and another group of lighter elements.

I adore trailing elements too: some stems of jasmine or maidenhair vine, or anything delicate with a natural drape that will move and float as the bride walks. These can be added in little dots throughout the bouquet, with a couple of larger stems at the end trailing off down one side.

When you are happy with the bouquet, secure the stems at the point where you hold them with some floral tape. Then tie a silk ribbon (raw, naturally dyed silk is my favourite) around the base to hide the tape. You can tie it off with either a simple knot, cutting the ribbon short, or make a flopsy bow, leaving the ribbon ends long, with one end longer than the other so that they sway when the bride walks. Froufrou Chic and Songbird Silk sell lovely hand-dyed silk ribbons.

Trim the stems of the bouquet so that they are even. My preference is for shorter stems that extend no more than 10 cm (4 in) below the bottom of the hand holding the arrangement.

The bridesmaids' bouquets can be a variation of the bride's, just a bit smaller. Not all identical, but using mostly the same materials.

Place the bouquets in shallow water (you don't want the ribbons to be dripping wet) and refrigerate them until you hand them over.

TOP

When you've arranged the bouquet, tie it off with floral tape and trim the stems so that they are level before placing the bouquet in water.

BOTTOM

A raw, naturally dyed silk ribbon is a wonderful way to finish off a bridal bouquet.

ON BOUTONNIERES

The boys' boutonnieres – a fancy word for the tiny clutch of flowers you pin onto the lapels of suits – are where you get a chance to channel any pixie leanings (we all have them, don't we?) and twist together the most minuscule, perfect ensemble of bits and pieces used in the wedding bouquets and other arrangements. Simple and small works best.

To make the boutonnieres – and I recommend making more than you need, just in case – you simply choose a few little pieces and bunch them together in-between your thumb and index finger. From there, wrap the stems with a piece of floral tape, then tie a ribbon around the stem and secure it with a single knot. Cut the ribbon ends short and on the diagonal so as to make a simple, almost bow-tie shape.

Trim the stems so that they are level. Attach a pin to the ribbon to use when you attach the boutonnieres later on.

Place them in a shallow tray of water and refrigerate them until they're needed.

Just before the service, pin the boutonnieres onto the left lapels of the groom and groomsmen. Hold the boutonniere in place with your non-dominant hand. Then, holding the pin with your other hand, fold the lapel over. Insert the pin through the back of the lapel, up and into the back of the ribbon, then up and out again through to the back of the lapel. Fold the lapel back into place, *et voila*.

Left: A tiny boutonniere made of flowering potato vine and fragrant pelargonium leaves.
Right: Boutonnieres made of dogwood flowers, paper daisies, little, light textural balls of love in a puff and dried gum leaves.

A BIG SPRING WEDDING

●

VENUE

Walcha, New England, New South Wales.
The ceremony was held on the groom's family farm in a paddock at the top of a hill,
with the reception in a glorious old woolshed nearby.

FOR THE CEREMONY

1 bridal bouquet

5 bridesmaids' bouquets

16 boutonnieres (for the groom, groomsmen and other wedding party members)

1 vase of peonies for the signing table

1 dogwood archway

12 mini meadow aisle explosions and 1 mini explosion for the base of the archway

FOR THE RECEPTION

5 clouds of dogwood and gum leaves for the ceiling beams

2 large arrangements of peonies, roses and crabapple branches for the bar

1 large urn of white roses, peonies and gum leaves for the entrance

18 small jars of garden roses for the tables inside

8 medium jars of peonies for the tables outside

Above: Cattle inspecting the site of the wedding ceremony – a small plateau on a hilltop, with 360 degree views of the valley below.
Right: The woolshed, where the reception was held.
Opposite: My trusty trailer filled with dogwood and other cuttings from Jules's garden.

Above & left: Picking paper daisies from the side of the road.
Opposite: Lugging buckets and bundles of dogwood branches and other garden treasures from the car to the woolshed, with help from the bride's father.

BUYING, PICKING AND PROCESSING

The bride bought $800 of peonies (about 60 bunches) from New England Peonies, a peony farm about half an hour's drive from the wedding venue. It was the end of the peony season, so we were lucky to get the generous amount that we did. The roses, dogwood and other bits and bobs came from Jules's garden, and I found the tiny paper daisies and the large branches of dried gum leaves on the side of the road.

I strongly recommend you have all the flowers and foliage picked and processed (by 'processed' I mean cleaning the stems of any unwanted leaves, removing any gnarly thorns, cutting stems on the diagonal before plunging them into buckets of clean water) at least one day before the wedding. This process is very time consuming and tiring – particularly if you have picked the flowers yourself – and it is important you give yourself enough time afterwards to bring it all together. You might think it won't take long, but it does.

Above: Cutting bundles and bundles of roses from Jules's garden the day before the wedding.
Right: Buckets of beautiful peonies sitting patiently in the cool shade of the woolshed.
Opposite: Behind the scenes. Making sure all flowers and branches are prepped and are happily sitting in fresh water before the arranging begins.

THE BOUQUETS

PEONIES, GARDEN ROSES, FLOWERING DOGWOOD, SMOKEBUSH

If I were to have a heart attack at any point in the lead-up to this
wedding, it would have been when I was making the bouquets.
I wanted the bride to love her bouquet so much; I wanted her to
look fabulous; I didn't want to stuff it up. Therefore I did, quite a
few times.

A few failed attempts and a cup of tea later, I decided to keep it
simple. I chose the most beautiful, open pink peonies of the lot,
some super fragrant garden roses, a floaty piece of dogwood and
some deep purple smokebush foliage for the base. That was it.
Joyful and exuberant, like the bride herself. I sat it in a cool place
in a bucket of water along with the bridesmaids' bouquets, which
were smaller variations on the same theme. The next day, I took the
bouquets out of their buckets, tied them with silk ribbons, placed
them in shallow water in individual glass cylindrical vases and took
them to the house where the girls were getting ready. It was such
an intimate moment, handing the flowers over to those beautiful,
excited girls.

The boutonnieres (page 161) were also kept simple: little clutches of
paper daisies, dogwood flowers, love in a puff and dried gum leaves.

Left: The bride and her mother on the wedding day, holding the bouquet made of dogwood flowers, fragrant garden roses, pink, fluffy peonies and smokebush leaves.
Above: The gorgeous bride and her delightful bridesmaids holding their colourful bouquets on the wedding day.

THE CEREMONY

MINI MEADOW EXPLOSIONS: *PEONIES, SMOKEBUSH, ACANTHUS, BUTTERFLY BUSH, WILD GRASSES, CAGED FLORAL FOAM BLOCKS, TENT PEGS*
THE ARBOUR: *FLOWERING DOGWOOD BRANCHES, ZIP TIES*
SIGNING TABLE: *PEONIES, A GLASS WECK JAR, ADHESIVE PUTTY*

For the ceremony in the paddock, I broke my usual floral foam ban and used double bricks of it in plastic cages for the bases of the mini meadow explosions that ran down the length of the aisle, on either side of the hay bale seating. It was a hot day and there was no running water on the hilltop, so I opted for pre-soaked floral foam. I kind of hate myself for it, but that's the truth of the matter.

We assembled the twelve blocks in the shade of the shed, spiking peonies, smokebush, acanthus spires, butterfly bush fronds and wild grasses into the floral foam, disguising the foam blocks with extra grass. We took them out to the ceremony in the back of the ute an hour before the service and sat them at the base of the hay bales.

It was windy as well as hot, so I made sure the blocks of mini meadows were secure by hammering tent pegs through the plastic cages and into the ground. I also stabilised the vase of peonies on the signing table, which kept wanting to fall over thanks to the wind, with a generous blob of adhesive putty. Always carry adhesive putty!

The groom had built a lovely wooden arbour. Around its base I added another mini meadow explosion, then zip-tied four branches of flowering dogwood to make it look as if it was growing up and out of the base.

Top: Zip-tying the dogwood branches to the wooden arbour the groom made for the hilltop ceremony.
Bottom: A simple glass Weck jar filled with peonies decorated the signing table. A big blob of adhesive putty at the base of the vase stopped it from being blown over by the wind.
Opposite: The aisle flanked by mini explosions of peonies, smokebush, acanthus, butterfly bush and wild grasses fixed into bricks of floral foam, secured in place with plastic cages and tent pegs.

THE RECEPTION

PEONIES, GARDEN ROSES, SMOKEBUSH, CRABAPPLE, FLOWERING DOGWOOD, DRIED GUM BRANCHES, CAGED FLORAL FOAM BLOCKS, ZIP TIES

The plan was to create waves of dried gum leaves suspended from the rafters of the old woolshed – all airy, with tonal browns, tans and greys – up high in the vast ceiling space. But when I saw the beautiful dogwood flowering, I knew it had to go up there too, with all its green leaves picked off so that it was just the four-petaled white flowers floating in among the bleached-out gum leaves. I think it is such an advantage if you can be flexible in situations like this; after all, if dogwood is flowering, use it! I would have just used zip ties to fix the gum tree branches to the beams, but because the dogwood flowers wilt easily, I zip-tied more of those awful pre-soaked blocks of floral foam in plastic cages to the tops of the beams and wedged the dogwood branches into those, giving extra support with more zip ties.

I kept the bright pops of colour provided by the roses and peonies at ground level, on the tables and sideboards, to mix in with the bridal bouquets and all the glittering glamour of the men and women in their black-tie party gear.

LARGE ARRANGEMENTS

LEFT: *CRABAPPLE BRANCHES, TALL STEMS OF ROSES, CHICKEN WIRE*
BELOW: *PEONIES, DOGWOOD BRANCHES, ROSES, DRIED GUM BRANCHES*

I made up two large arrangements in a pair of wonderful footed zinc buckets from Jules's collection for the bar area in the shed. I cannot tell you how much I wanted to steal those buckets. Filled with crabapple branches, towering rose stems and peonies, all angled into chicken wire, they were such a great size for a room of these proportions. The arrangements looked both large and delicate, and so beautiful against the muted wooden walls of the shed.

For the entrance, I filled a concrete urn with white peonies, dogwood branches, white roses and dried, bleached-out gum branches: a ground-floor echo of what was happening at the ceiling up above. Never be scared of repetition in an event like this – it brings a much-welcomed sense of cohesiveness.

A SMALL, WHITE AUTUMN WEDDING

●

VENUE

The woolshed and shearers' quarters of a sheep and cattle farm in the beautiful Dumaresq Valley, north-west New South Wales.

FOR THE WEDDING

1 bridal bouquet

1 cotton installation for the reception

1 tableau for the verandah in the nearby shearers' quarters

3 small arrangements for the bathrooms and kitchen

Cotton is the most fabulous plant material to use for installations. When it is ready to pick, it is effectively dead: the leaves have all fallen off, the stems are dry, and the buds have well and truly burst open, their Dr Seuss-like cotton balls spilling out. Hence, cotton does not need to sit in water to stay looking good. You can zip-tie bunches of cotton to beams in old sheds and leave them there for months, if you wish, and they will continue to look fabulous.

My husband grows cotton, as do many of his friends. Large cotton-picking machines rip through the paddocks every autumn, cutting the stems, separating the cotton buds from them and balling up the cotton into huge, round 2.2-tonne bails. To get the cotton when it is still on its stem, you need to get to it before the cotton pickers do, with secateurs and an empty ute tray in which to pile your cuttings.

When farmers sell their cotton all bailed up as a commodity, they get paid about 60 cents a square metre of crop. So if you befriend a cotton farmer (which I suggest you do), flutter your eyelashes and offer to pay them a good deal more, I am sure some of them will be happy to let you come and pick as many square metres as you can.

Then all you need to do is find an old shed and *voila*, you have almost everything you need for a small, intimate wedding for twenty guests.

THE BOUQUET

COTTON BRANCHES, ICEBERG ROSES, CACTUS DAHLIAS, SHASTA DAISY, EVENING PRIMROSE, PELARGONIUM, FLOWERING POTATO VINE

Because the arrangement in the shed was restricted to cotton and cotton alone, I thought it would be lovely if the bouquet was also white, but full of softer elements and textures. The trailing potato vines in particular added a very feminine, delicate touch to the bouquet. And of course, the fragrance from the roses and the pelargoniums was just delightful.

THE RECEPTION

COTTON BRANCHES, ZIP TIES

The cotton cloud above the reception table was made using the same principles as the overhead kitchen cotton installation (page 133). While you are on ground level, create a number of bunches of cotton – some big, some small – and tie them off at the stems with zip ties. Then climb up a ladder and, one by one, attach the bunches to the beam with more zip ties or string, creating an undulating wave down its length, running parallel above the table. You want some bunches to point up, others to point sideways, others to point outwards. Remember, you are aiming for a three-dimensional shape with different heights and depths.

THE TABLEAU & SMALL ARRANGEMENTS

ABOVE: *PUMPKINS, PRICKLY PEAR, OLIVE LEAVES, DRIED HYDRANGEAS, TULIPS,*
PEPPER LEAVES
OPPOSITE: *ROSE BRANCHES*

A tableau on the verandah of the shearers' quarters using pumpkins, a potted
prickly pear, an enamel jug filled with olive leaves, dried hydrangeas, tulips and
pepper leaves and a rusty bucket of various branches, all arranged at different
heights and depths. The iceberg roses in the black bucket on the left were destined
for smaller vases in the bedrooms behind. A simple glass bottle filled with three
stems of fragrant roses decorated the humble bathroom.

Poppies for sale at the Sydney Flower Market.

A TRIP TO THE FLOWER MARKET

•

I recently went to the Sydney flower market with a florist friend. I'd happily never go there again.

She had casually warned, 'Oh, there's a chance I might have a panic attack' but I thought that, because this is somewhere she goes regularly for work, she was just being funny.

I met her in the rooftop carpark at 4.30 am on a Friday morning. Already, all the car spots were taken. I started lapping the carpark, along with several other harried-looking women, until a text came from my friend advising me to 'pull over and create your own parking spot'. So I did, though not without some angst.

As I locked my car in its non-carpark, a desperate lady in a tiny car, who had also been lapping, pulled up alongside me and stuck her head out of her open window. 'Where can I park? Why do they charge us $10 to get into the carpark if there are no spaces? At 4.30 in the morning?'

I told her – calmly, as if I was a regular, 'You must make your own, anywhere you think you can get away with'.

Without a word, she put her window up and drove off. This was the atmosphere in the pre-dawn darkness of that Friday morning.

I met my friend at the lift. She had parked her hired van in another dodgy spot (this is a great tip for flower market amateurs like me: hire a van for the day if you plan on getting any significant quantity of flowers. Also bring big, rectangular plastic tubs filled less than a quarter full with water. Round buckets will tip over as soon as you hit the first speed bump on the way out). Thankfully, I had a four-wheel drive, unlike that poor woman in her small vehicle.

We made our way down to the flower market below and lined up at the shut roller doors. Not even at the main ones, but at a less obvious one set at the side that still had at least twelve people milling around, not talking, but occasionally peering through the slits in the door to spy whatever it was they were going to make a sprint for when the doors opened.

At 5 am the roller doors began to come up, and I am not lying when I say that people crouched under the gap as the doors opened and ran for their dogwood blossoms, or whatever it was they were worried they were going to miss. It was like being in a dystopian movie where petrified florists have to find the perfect cherry blossom branch, of which there is a limited amount, or face death.

I am pleased to report my friend didn't crouch and run, but she sure did power-walk through those aisles of flower stalls. Everyone looked stressed to me: the growers and the buyers. The market forces of supply and demand, as told through flowers – spectacular flowers. The produce was astounding, but all morning I was plagued by the feeling that I was missing out on very important things. Exactly what, I was not sure.

Plus, I was wearing long flares that brushed the ground and soaked up water like a sponge. The floor of the flower market is wet. Don't wear flares, even if you do think they look flattering when you catch a glimpse of yourself in the mirror at 3 am before leaving the house.

From what I could see, the market morning was broken up into three distinct sessions: the first session is all business, where you run around saying, 'I'll take that, that and that'. You power-walk down the aisles, check out the different stalls and put your name on the stuff you want, saying to the grower that you'll be back.

Once you've secured your picks, you shift into the second session, which is all about returning to the growers, paying them in cash and being nice to them to strengthen your relationship for future first sessions.

Session three is the take-it-to-the-car session. This involves either lots of little trips holding as many bunches as you can from the marketplace to the lift, up the lift and to your car, which may or may not have been towed away, with your wet flares slapping your ankles. Or one or two more intense trips with a borrowed trolley, dodging Bobcats with flashing lights. There are lots of tiered trolleys around. I am not actually sure who owns them or how you get one, but I know it has something to do with being nice to the growers or spending incredible amounts of money.

The morning was far too intense for me. I was hungry, cold and a long way from home. My friend didn't have a panic attack, but I'll tell you what, I was close. I would happily leave this experience to the professionals and arrive at the markets at 8.30 am, when the parking is easy, to pick over whatever flowers are left. Or just take my chances with whatever is growing next to the railway track.

There is also something inherently stressful about having so much choice. The markets have everything, and it all looks spectacular. It's very hard to come away with a curated selection of flowers and foliage when the pool from which to choose is so vast and so good. This editing process is a skill in and of itself, and I would very much rather nature do it for me.

So if you do find yourself doing the flowers for an event, by all means go to the markets to get your material. But be warned: no small cars, no silly little buckets and no flares. Bring lots of cash, friends with helping hands and a steely focus. All this while the rest of the city sleeps.

Buckets brimming with flowering dogwood lilac and cherry blossoms, and shelves of paper-wrapped fragrant roses at the Sydney Flower Market.

A glass cylindrical vase on a stool, filled with branches of pink magnolia and plum blossoms, brings a moment of joy to the church entrance for this funeral service.

A FUNERAL

•

'I bought some tulips for my grandmother's grave … and I had them sitting on the potting bench at Dixter. When I turned my back he planted them in the long border. I said to him "Christo, those are for my grandmother's grave!" And he said, "Oh, she doesn't need them, she's dead".'

- GREAT DIXTER HEAD GARDENER FERGUS GARRETT ON HIS BOSS, THE LEGENDARY, CANTANKEROUS GARDEN WRITER CHRISTOPHER LLOYD

I live a very secular life, where traditions and rituals come in the form of Friday night drinks with the neighbours. But in extreme circumstances, like the death of someone I love, it is to the traditional rituals of organised religion that I immediately turn.

A funeral, a coffin, a reading, a wake. I wouldn't know what else to do. And in my case, because of my Anglo background, flowers are a crucial part of it. Flowers are a way to honour the dead and comfort the grieving. If having flowers at a funeral is part of your cultural history too, I hope the following will be of use, should you need it.

If you do find yourself in this position, you are no doubt sad enough. You do not need to be further depressed by the idea of choosing a $400 casket spray from the floral sympathy section of a funeral catalogue. The sight of lilies and carnations stuck into a brick of floral foam on top of someone I love dearly could shift me from a state of denial to one of unbridled rage. Maybe having the flowers organised as quickly as possible would be a relief to you, but I could not bear to inject such ugliness into the situation. Beauty scatters the seeds of hope in us, as Sister Joan Chittister says, and for me that beauty means no bricks of floral foam, no fake doves and no casket sprays.

None of which, by the way, are compulsory. You can do what you like, even if that is piling a heap of loose flowers on the coffin.

'Due to PTSD I can't remember what we did for my mum's funeral,' said a friend whom I trust with all things floral – actually, with all things. 'But at a friend's mum's, we just put flowers all over the casket because she wanted them to roll off as they wheeled it out. She had been sick for a while. That's one benefit of knowing you are dying. Creative control.'

Alternatively, you can make a bunch of flowers and foliage, tied together with a ribbon or a piece of string. The funeral director might sit the bunch on a small non-slip mat on top of the coffin, or straight on top of the coffin. Or you can make a little raft of branches woven together with string and then fix your flowers to that. Or just leave it at the branches. Wouldn't a couple of branches of flowering dogwood on top of the coffin be simple and lovely?

To me, the point of decorating a coffin with flowers is to inject a note of tenderness and softness into the stark reality that is the sight of a coffin holding someone you recently had a cup of tea with.

The act of doing the flowers yourself allows you an opportunity to grieve and to think about and honour the person who has died through the simple, common framework of flowers. The immediate family may be too overwhelmed to do it, but a group of close friends could offer to handle it.

If you are going to do the flowers for the funeral of someone you love, under no circumstance are you to put any pressure on yourself to make the flowers look 'amazing'. This is not about wowing the crowd. This is about the ritual more than the result. The act of remembrance, not of ego. After all, your beloved friend is certainly not going to complain.

You can choose the flowers from a shop, keeping your friend in mind as you look through the buckets, remembering or even guessing what she would like. Or you could snip some bits and pieces from her garden, a place where she can no longer get about in her crocs. Or from your garden, if you have one, or the street or neighbourhood in which she lived. All the while, you are thinking about her through the limited perspective of flowers. Anything else might be too much to bear at this point. You can then stand around a table, or under a favourite tree, with daughters and mothers and aunts and friends to arrange the flowers for this lost person, together. It can be a beautiful shared ritual: a small ballast to clutch onto in the hideous loneliness of grief. And if you pick or buy what is in season, each year at the same time those flowers will come out and remind you of your friend.

I want to be buried in the simplest cardboard coffin available, under a tree at home, if I can organise the proper paperwork. I want the coffin to be covered in whatever is growing at the time – big bunches of floating clematis vines, or flowering apple blossoms, or roses or dahlias, or beautiful wattle and gum and fennel from the side of the road. Just a generous pile of whatever is abundant.

We buried a little dog of ours under a young Chinese elm tree, and the tree is growing with vigour. I would like my body to be able to do the same for another tree: to feed the worms and enrich the soil. Where I live you can apply to the local authority for permission to be buried on private land, as long as it is more than 5 hectares. If you like the idea of being buried under a tree, but do not like the idea of being buried on private land (it will more than likely be sold down the track) or do not live on more than 5 hectares, natural burial grounds are worth looking into, and they are becoming more common.

I have really got off topic here, but I do think it is good to talk about this part of life that is so often kept behind closed doors. Now, back to the flowers.

DECORATING THE COFFIN

WATTLE BRANCHES, ROSEMARY, BAY LEAVES, MAIDENHAIR VINE, STRING, CAGED BLOCK OF FLORAL FOAM (IF YOU WISH)

It is common for florists to build a 'casket spray' – a block of floral foam with flowers and foliage sticking out from every side, except of course the bottom – to place on top of the coffin. To me, they often look incredibly static. Like a newsreader's hair that remains perfectly in place despite the howling wind that is causing everything around her to flap while she does her reporting.

If you want to use a floral foam base, try to include trailing elements – vines, pendulous foliage, delicate flowers on long stems – so that the arrangement has a natural movement as the coffin is wheeled or carried towards its final destination.

A FOAMLESS ARRANGEMENT

For this large arrangement (about 2 m/6.5 ft long), I used wattle branches to make a base upon which the rest of the foliage could sit.

Line up three slender branches, about 1 m (3 ft) in length, and strip the leaves off the lower 30 cm (12 in). Then lay two smaller sticks or stems perpendicularly across the three branches, forming a grid. Tie the grid together with string at the points at which they intersect, creating a raft-like base. Repeat the process with another three branches to make another raft.

Set up the wattle base on something that is easy to work on – an ironing board is terrific – with one raft pointing to the left and the other pointing right, their stems meeting in the middle. This will form the base that will sit on the coffin. Building it in two parts – the right half and the left half – will make it easier to transport.

On top of each half, add in bunches of rosemary, bay leaves and more wattle, interspersed with trailing lengths of maidenhair vine, and secure them to the base with string, wire or zip ties. Imagine building up each raft so that they seem to explode out to either side.

When it comes time to place it on the coffin (feel free to put a non-slip mat on the coffin top), overlap the raft bases and secure them together with string, wire or zip ties. Add more sprigs of rosemary and wattle to create some height in the middle of the arrangement.

This funeral raft can very happily sit out of water for a day or two.

A raft of wattle, bay leaves, rosemary and maidenhair vine for a coffin. For ease of transport, it helps to build the two halves separately and then join them together in situ.

SIMPLE BUNCHES FOR THE COFFIN

BELOW: *VIRGINIA CREEPER, NASTURTIUM, DRIED SEED HEADS*
OPPOSITE: *ICEBERG ROSES, CYCLAMEN, ROSEMARY*

If you like, you can simply place a bunch of flowers on top of the coffin. Here are two options, both quite lightweight. I would avoid using anything particularly heavy, just in case it falls off.

Above: A simple, lightweight, trailing bunch of nasturtium, Virginia creeper and dried seed heads make up this autumnal bouquet for a coffin.
Opposite: Iceberg roses, pink cyclamen, purple clematis and a sprig of rosemary for remembrance create a feminine bouquet.

A CHURCH SERVICE

THE COFFIN: *MAGNOLIA, HELLEBORES, JONQUILS, PEPPER TREE LEAVES*
LARGE ARRANGEMENTS: *SPRING BLOSSOMS, HELLEBORES*

A funeral can be beautiful. It is not, unfortunately, a wedding. Nevertheless, a church can be filled with fragrant flowers and delicate blossoms to inject some loveliness into the room.

Here, a plywood coffin is almost blanketed by a large bunch of magnolias, pink and cream hellebores, fragrant jonquils and the trailing leaves of the pepper tree. I used a double brick of floral foam, soaked in water, sitting in a plastic tray for the base of the arrangement on top of the coffin. Hellebores and magnolias can wilt quickly, and I did not want to risk sad, droopy flowers for the service.

Around the coffin and throughout the church are big, joyous bunches of spring blossoms and hellebores. In your arrangement, use the principles of flower arrangement from the Flower Basics chapter (page 17), and let some foliage and flowers spill over your vessel. The ceilings of churches are often high, so don't be afraid to go for some scale in your arrangements.

I found all this new, floral life around the coffin incredibly moving. Our own lives may come to an end, but the cycle of nature goes around and around. Winter is always followed by spring.

It can be a lovely idea to bring a tree into the church. You can find all sorts of trees in nurseries whose root balls are bagged up in lightweight sacks that make them relatively easy to transport. Wheel the tree in on a trolley and cover the plastic root ball bag with hessian or linen, or surround it with spring blossoms (pictured here, on the right of the coffin). After the service, the family can plant the tree in honour of your friend at a place of their choosing.

FLOWER TOOLKIT

SEASONAL FLOWER ARRANGING GUIDE

•

This list serves as a guide for what flowers you can expect to find at different times of the year. If you are putting together a fancy arrangement in a vase, you'll want to start with foliage, then think about adding floral elements from any of these categories: several large focal flowers, several smaller focal flowers, perhaps some trailing elements, tall flowers or flowering branches. Within this list, you can create many combinations; some will work better than others. It is up to you to decide how many categories you want to include in your arrangement.

You already know how much I love a simple bunch made up of only large focal flowers. But equally, imagine an urn bursting with peonies (large focal flowers), anemones (small focal flowers), sweet peas (delicate and textural), branches of mock orange (flowering and fruiting branches) and trailing jasmine (trailing plants and vines) spilling over the edge. Sounds good to me.

	SPRING	SUMMER	AUTUMN	WINTER
FOCAL FLOWERS, LARGE	cattleya orchid	artichoke flowers	chrysanthemum	camellia
	guelder rose (*Viburnum opulus*)	carnation	cotton	cattleya orchid
	hippeastrum	dahlia	dahlia	magnolia
	lily	giant aster	hydrangea	phalaenopsis orchid
	magnolia	hydrangea	rose	protea
	peony	lily	sunflower	
	phalaenopsis orchid	lotus		
	ranunculus	evergreen magnolias, and in particular *Magnolia grandiflora*		
	rose	rose		
	waratah	sunflower		
FOCAL FLOWERS, SMALLER	anemone (spring-flowering varieties such as *Anemone coronaria*)	agapanthus	buddleia	orchid, such as cymbidium
	bearded iris	amaryllis	everlasting daisy	daphne
	cymbidium orchid	aster	Japanese anemone	hellebore
	daffodil and jonquil	buddleia	pelargonium	leucadendron
	daphne	calla lily	rudbeckia	
	hyacinth	English daisy	shasta daisy	
	iris	everlasting daisy	strawflower (*Xerochrysum bracteatum*)	
	lilac	frangipani		
	poppy	gardenia		
	tulip	orchid, such as phalaenopsis		
		pelargonium		
		rudbeckia		
		strawflower (*Xerochrysum bracteatum*)		
		waterlily		
		zinnia		

	SPRING	SUMMER	AUTUMN	WINTER
DELICATE AND TEXTURAL FLOWERS	allium	allium	baby's breath (*Gypsophila* spp.)	clematis seed heads
	baby's breath (*Gypsophila* spp.)	asparagus fronds	clematis seed heads	dried grass seed heads
	banksia rose	baby's breath (*Gypsophila* spp.)	grass seed heads	dried Russian sage
	bluebell	begonia	honesty seed pods	gumnut
	columbine	Christmas bush	peppercorn berry	honesty seed pods
	crocus	cosmos	rose hip	rose hip
	flannel flower	crocosmia	Russian sage	viola and violet
	freesia	grass seed heads	salvia	
	fritillaria	flowering tobacco	yarrow (*Achillea millefolium*)	
	Geraldton wax	lavender		
	lily-of-the-valley	nigella		
	nigella	pansy		
	paper daisy	phlox		
	salvia	Russian sage		
	snowdrop	scabiosa		
	sweet pea	statice		
	tea tree (*Leptospermum* spp.)	tea tree (*Leptospermum* spp.)		
		tuberose		
		yarrow (*Achillea millefolium*)		
FLOWERING AND FRUITING BRANCHES	dogwood	apricot, cherry, peach, plum	apple, pomegranate, quince	banksia
	flowering fruit blossoms, such as apple, cherry, crabapple, orange, pear, quince	fig	chestnut, hazelnut, pecan	citrus
	May bush (*Spiraea cantoniensis*)	fruiting blackberry, blueberry and raspberry		wattle
	mock orange (*Philadelphus* spp.)	smoke bush		
TALL FLOWERS	delphinium	amaranthus	delphinium (second flush)	
	larkspur	fennel	fennel	
	lupin	foxglove	Queen Anne's lace	
	stock	Queen Anne's lace		

	SPRING	SUMMER	AUTUMN	WINTER
VINES AND TRAILING PLANTS	bougainvillea	Boston ivy, Virginia creeper	Boston ivy, Virginia creeper (autumn coloured)	ivy
	clematis	bougainvillea	clematis	maidenhair vine
	honeysuckle	climbing roses such as 'Cecile Brunner'	ivy	
	ivy	honeysuckle	maidenhair vine	
	jasmine	hoya		
	maidenhair vine	ivy		
	wisteria	Madagascar jasmine (*Stephanotis floribunda*)		
		maidenhair vine		
		nasturtium		
		passionfruit vine		
		star jasmine		

A WORD ON FOLIAGE

•

Evergreen foliage such as olive, gum, oak, wattle, heuchera and some magnolias are available all year, whereas other favourite foliage plants, including smoke bush, lose their leaves in winter. Bracken and ferns are available all year if you don't mind using the dried wintery leaves, which I actually prefer to the fresh ones.

When choosing foliage, opt for branches that have curves and movement in them rather than the straight up-and-down stems. It is much easier to create natural arrangements when you start with a foliage base that has movement and curves.

FAVOURITE FLOWERS BY SEASON

●

Back in the 17th century, when the availability of flowers on offer was limited by season and geography, the idealised bunch of flowers painted by the Dutch and Flemish masters – in which you would see impossible combinations of flowers from all seasons in the same vase – was revered. Now, when you can get a wide range of flowers any time of the year, it feels much more luxurious to use local and seasonal options.

SPRING

allium

anemone (the spring kind)

aquilegia (columbine, granny's bonnet)

blossoms (apple, cherry, crabapple, orange, pear, plum)

clematis

daffodil

dogwood

fennel fronds, green

flannel flower

foxglove

freesia

fritillaria

gardenia

hyacinth

iris

jasmine

lilac

magnolia

mock orange (*Philadelphus* spp.)

peony

poppy

ranunculus

rose

snowball viburnum

sweet pea

tulip

wisteria

SUMMER

allium

basil

buddleia

campanula

carnation

clematis

daisy

delphinium

fennel

foxglove

geranium/pelargonium

hoary stock

hydrangea

nasturtium

passionflower vine

AUTUMN

achillea

apples on branches

aster

autumn leaves

chestnut branches and flowers

chrysanthemum

clematis and seed heads

cotton

fig

fuchsia

hydrangea

passionflower vine

pecan

pepper tree branches and seeds

sedum

sunflower

WINTER

branches

columbine leaves

cotton

forced bulb blossoms

hellebore

honesty seed pods

hydrangea, dried

magnolia

orchid

ALL YEAR

eucalyptus

mistletoe

rosemary

sage

PLANTS THAT LAST
WELL OUT OF WATER

●

Generally speaking, the older, woodier and tougher the stem is, the longer it will last out of water. Waxy leaves also indicate a propensity to last well without water. As a rule, you can't go wrong with perennial shrubs native to Australia and South Africa, and of course eucalyptus leaves. Tough as old boots. But other flowers, such as orchids, lilies, roses and chrysanthemums are very robust too, as is the foliage from magnolias, olives, oaks, rosemary, thyme, box (buxus), ferns and tropical plants like monstera and palm.

FOLIAGE

autumn leaves on stems

bay

blueberry leaves

box (buxus)

citrus foliage

ferns

gum

magnolia

maidenhair vine

monstera

olive

palm leaves, particularly the ruffled fan palm leaves

pelargonium

pepper tree

persimmons on branch (when fruit is close to ripe)

raspberry leaves

rosemary

Russian sage

sage

smoke bush

spring blossom branches

succulents

thyme

wattle

FLOWERS

artichoke

baby's breath (*Gypsophila*)

banksia

cardoon

carnation

chrysanthemum

cornflower

cotton

crocosmia

everlasting daisy

fennel (not young)

geranium/pelargonium

globe thistle (*Echinops* spp.)

hydrangeas
(late-autumn and, of course, dried)

lily

protea

Queen Anne's lace (not young)

roses, not anywhere near blown (the banksia rose lasts well)

salvia (wooden ones, such as *Salvia involucrata* 'Bethellii'

sea holly (*Eryngium* spp.)

sedum

statice

strawflowers

wattle in blossom

yarrow (*Achillea millefolium*)

FLOWERS
(ESPECIALLY IF HUNG UPSIDE DOWN)

delphinium

larkspur

sunflower

GRASSES

miscanthus

pampas

SEED PODS

allium

gumnuts

honesty

poppy

raintree foliage

NOTORIOUS WILTERS

anything with new growth

hellebore

hollyhock

hydrangea, fresh

lilac

magnolia flowers

prunus foliage (almond, apricot, cherry, nectarine, peach, plum)

FLOWER THINGS I SIMPLY REFUSE TO DO

•

Sear the ends of poppy stems with a naked flame. I know people swear by this method to keep poppies looking good for longer, but I cannot bring myself to do it. And besides, the ever-faithful CSIRO *Caring for Cut Flowers* guide makes a pretty clear case for bypassing the scalding method. (To be read in an authoritative, but non-judgemental satellite-navigator voice): 'Scalding is an inexact process and often results in damage to stem ends: the stems curl up and form a U-shape, which severely hinders water uptake.'

Delicately slice the stems of hellebores lengthwise with a razor blade and float in water before putting in a vase to prolong their life. I know I will never do this. Ever. Just pick older hellebores that have done away with stamens and formed seed pods in their place. Also, the darker hellebores seem to last longer.

Hairspray anything to keep its seed heads/blossoms intact. Actually, I would take this one a step further and just say no to hairspraying anything.

Use floral foam. I have used floral foam, but it really is hideous, powdery stuff. Chicken wire is a very capable understudy, and has the advantage of not causing cancer.

Say the term 'casket spray' or 'sympathy flowers' out loud. Times are already sad enough.

INDEX

•

Italicised numbers indicate images.

Above: A wooden pail brimming with autumn leaves in the shed.
Right: Supermarket-bought baby's breath (*Gypsophila*) makes for
a textural, delicate and very long-lasting arrangement in this old
corrugated iron bathroom.

ABOUT THE AUTHOR

Annabelle Hickson is a self-taught florist who lives on a pecan farm on the New South Wales–Queensland border in Australia with her husband and three children. She worked as a news journalist at *The Australian* newspaper before she was lured out to the countryside by a handsome farmer. She now creates floral installations and teaches classes on how to do the flowers worldwide. Follow her on Instagram @annabellehickson

ACKNOWLEDGEMENTS

'Every book is, in an intimate sense, a circular letter to the friends of him who writes it ... they find private messages, assurances of love, and expressions of gratitude, dropped for them in every corner.'

- ROBERT LOUIS STEVENSON

This book is a love letter to a handful of people who have helped directly and indirectly. I hope you enjoy the private messages and assurances of love dropped in for you throughout the pages. Special thanks to Caitlin Melling and Fiona Bateman, for scattering the seeds of beauty wherever you go, and to Luisa Brimble, for showing me how to find them. To Mum, for teaching me, from the very beginning, that creating beauty is a thing worth doing. And to Ed, for introducing me to the wonders of life beyond the city walls.

I am eternally grateful to Flore Vallery-Radot, Luisa Brimble, Pip Williams and Anna Tomlinson for not only generously giving their time to take additional photos for this book, but for also giving me permission to use their lovely work in these pages.

Heartfelt thanks to the following friends who have opened up their homes and sheds and gardens, and let me in with secateurs and zip ties and cameras. Mandy Reid from The White Cottage – you have given me so much, my friend – thank you. Julia and Philip Harpham, Flore Vallery-Radot, Steve Haslam and Bianca Wicks, Sophie Hansen, Kimmie and Sandy Cameron, Jules Young, Michelle Conkas, Lean Timms and Sophie and Simon Wright.

The joy of working with a publishing team made up of people who are very good at what they do has been immensely satisfying. Thank you to Hardie Grant, and to Jane Willson for having faith in this book. To Anna Collett for turning a series of rambling word documents into a proper book. To Kate Armstrong for sensitively shaping the words so that they actually made sense, and to Andy Warren and his brilliant eye for bringing the design of this book to life. And thank you to Emiko Davies for introducing me to Hardie Grant.

And most of all to Ed, Daisy, Tom and Harriet. For putting up with so much. But most importantly for making my life out in the bush feel so full and rich.

This edition published in 2024 by Hardie Grant Books, an imprint of Hardie Grant Publishing
First published in 2019

Hardie Grant Books (Melbourne)
Building 1, 658 Church Street
Richmond, Victoria 3121

Hardie Grant Books (London)
5th & 6th Floors
52–54 Southwark Street
London SE1 1UN

hardiegrantbooks.com/books

Hardie Grant acknowledges the Traditional Owners of the Country on which we work, the Wurundjeri
People of the Kulin Nation and the Gadigal People of the Eora Nation, and recognises their continuing
connection to the land, waters and culture. We pay our respects to their Elders past and present.

A catalogue record for this
book is available from the
National Library of Australia

A Tree in the House
ISBN 978 1 74379 985 7

10 9 8 7 6 5 4 3 2 1

Publishing Director: Jane Willson
Managing Editor: Marg Bowman
Project Editor: Anna Collett
Editor: Kate J. Armstrong
Design Manager: Jessica Lowe
Designer: Andy Warren
Photographers: Annabelle Hickson, Edward Hickson, Pip Williams, Michelle Conkas, Luisa Brimble,
Anna Tomlinson, Flore Vallery-Radot
Production Manager: Todd Rechner

Colour reproduction by Splitting Image Colour Studio
Printed in China by Leo Paper Product LTD.

The paper this book is printed on is from FSC®-certified forests and other
sources. FSC® promotes environmentally responsible, socially beneficial
and economically viable management of the world's forests.

Annabelle Hickson would like to acknowledge the following people/locations for kindly granting permission for photography: Sophie Hansen family
farm, Rydal, Australia (pages 108, 109); Flore Vallery-Radot family château, Burgundy, France (pages 118–119, 121–122, 140, 142–143);
Mandy Reid, The White Cottage Flower Farm, Tenterfield, Australia (pages 124, 149); The Old Convent, Orange, Australia (pages 129–131);
Lean Timms, The Wild Food Supper (pages 144, 145); Steve Haslan & Bianca Wicks, Tenterfield, Australia (pages 192, 200–201).
Thank you also to Sarah Glover for the wedding cake (page 181), and to Caitlin Melling for her help with styling (pages 184–186).

All attempts were made to contact the copyright holders of the quotes and excerpts used in this book, and Annabelle Hickson would like to thank
and acknowledge the authors and publishers of these works.